Where Is My Magic?

Where Is My Magic?

BEYOND SELF ESTEEM

Joanne Salsbury

ISBN: 0692365648
ISBN 13: 9780692365649

Introduction

I dedicate this book to all who have lost hope that magic still exists! I have committed my life figuring out where my magic went and feel I can relay my experiences and knowledge in a way that unlock dreams into manifestation. We have become afraid to allow hope in because of doubt that we deserve more than we have been told we can achieve. It requires a look into the past and not everyone is ready; but in time, everyone will be ready!

We can maintain a narrow focus or see the universe existing in ways that, to date, have entertained us only in movies. There are so many that feel stuck in life's circumstances and the magic for changing all of this actually resides in you! The new world requires you to take responsibility for what makes you whole and allow the past perspectives as learning options for change; not dictation of more inherited doubts and fears that keep you stuck.

I chose the cover picture because it represents exactly how I see life! It has a mystical aura that encompasses steps of learning. In the beginning, learning is represented by thicker books and as we go up the steps of knowledge, the road becomes much smoother and easier to walk if we grow appropriately. Along the way are orbs of light to give us just enough enlightenment without giving the final chapter completely away. You can see and visualize the scent of fresh air and know dawn is close. All with the anticipation of a new unknown over the horizon!

I have taken a few risks with this book by including some topics that some may feel too far out for them and may even wonder how it connects to self-esteem. I believe everything connects and nothing is out of the realm of imagination. Imagination had to come from somewhere☺ Are we reliving what already has been or can we see the future? I am not writing any of my words to change your thinking, but to expand the mind to possibilities!

"Cherish your visions and your dreams as they are
the children of your soul,
The blueprints of your ultimate achievements."
Napoleon Hill

Also Author of :
"The Many Faces of Self Esteem" Book 1
"Obtaining The Pearl"   Book 2

Website: http://joannesalsburyauthor.com/

Facebook: https://www.facebook.com/joannesalsburyauthor

Joanne is educated in Qigong healing methods used for the past 2000 years as a part of Chinese Medicine. She focuses on meta-acupuncture to assist self-healing.
See Website for services offered.

Table of Contents

CHAPTER 1

New Opportunities

...Even though you may feel intimidated
or unqualified to move to the next
level, be assured heaven is reaching its
hand through the window, guiding
and protecting you as you soar
upward... Unknown Author

New opportunities can appear from a mask of "loss" in which you are about to gain something even more exciting if you flow with it and not fight it! It can materialize as a new business proposal after loss of a job; a new idea enters your mind to follow a different path or an investment opportunity presents itself. You hear a song on the radio, see a magazine picture that sparks your attention, or a TV program blurts an answer out that you needed to hear at that moment. It could be that answer to a difficult learning lesson which has been a continued pattern of distress for many years.

We have heard this all before, but I feel it is worth reminding you now because we have a tendency to forget the silver linings and gifts provided by the universe. You may have stumbled on this book or someone mentioned it to you. Whatever the reason...Welcome! I hope you can relate and enjoy my journey. My goal is to expand your thinking, not change you with empty words. Of course, you need to transform yourself, but we will ponder the silver linings, dream about the unknowns, and create magic that has been lost!

I talk about "letting go" in Chapter 20 of my first book *The Many Faces of Self Esteem*. This is probably the most difficult thing to do because we have inherited most of our views for perhaps generations and continue to manifest the same results from information we learned as "fact" due to loyalty of family tradition. Humans are basically loyal to the family circle and their beliefs. Why not, we say? Many cultures prize their elderly and the wisdom accumulated over the years. It makes sense! Even with generations of wisdom at our fingertips, we do not usually have someone pointing out the generational dysfunctions and yet we continue to have belief in these aspects as well because it is the whole package. So where do we begin to unravel what is theirs and what needs to be ours?

We are already in times now when we need to come into our own truth and realize we do not want or need to be told how to live, think or act. We are tired of being used, abused and socially unaccepted in others' minds. It is becoming necessary to trust our own intuition about the direction of our life and how to live it. Learning to say NO will begin to feel good, setting boundaries will make you feel safe; unsavory and unhealthy negative people will begin to fall away from your life. Thoughts become clearer with colors, sounds and smells that will begin to reappear in a more refreshing coverlet around you. The old ways are gone! Accepting another's word for truth is not going to make it truth in our personal future. It is our responsibility to make things happen and who better to know you than you?

As per my experience, hunches will nag you about another's hidden agenda and intuitively these agendas will resonate oddly within you. Trust in those silent voices that attempt to guide you and start investigating those potentially purposeless words for yourself. Sometimes we don't want to hear what our intuition says or maybe we are not ready for that information yet, but your intuition wants you to face the reality of your and others' insecurities and unhealthy boundaries. We all have insecurities, but we miss opportunities when we allow the insecurities to take the lead. You can ignore them and continue to let untruths fester inside of you which will eventually affect your health over time or you can face the truth and release the energy obstruction that holds you in captivity. Your physical body will be your mirror.

Sometimes we feel trapped by outside circumstances whether it is financial, an unsatisfactory job, poor relationships or a spouse who tries to control any activity that will enhance growth. Some people have addictions they battle that resurface when things fall apart. It could simply be allowing others to manipulate your life and you manifest unwanted needs by their dictation of your every move. You actually have created these scenarios whether you believe it or not.   It is all still by your design.

Taking responsibility for the world you live in and the part you play in creating it is a new way of thinking to this generation, believe it or not, even though it is not new thinking. We have counted on external circumstances to guide our directions for centuries and where has that landed us? ...in depression, confusion, addictive relapse, divorce, wars and to some it is so over-whelming they take their lives. Getting unbound or unstuck from this lack of self responsibility takes many steps for inner growth to occur. We get stuck in thoughts of limitation noticeable by comments like "this is not possible", "this is not allowed", and "this will go wrong". Hence we fall deeper into our own creation of making that very thing happen. You become bound by the limited experience of others layered with your own limited experience which is usually "spawned by them originally" and it becomes a "never-ending" cycle.

Promises we make to ourselves with failure to fol-low through will cause us to have less trust in our decisions. We become angry with ourselves and our own credibility diminishes. This means low-ered self-esteem. Lower self-esteem leads to poor judgment, doubts in our decision making and can lead to depression if we keep doing the same thing over and over. We feel others may not trust our word and we feel less confident in ourselves to fol-low through convincingly. We can often appear untrustworthy to others and even grow to distrust ourselves. We start to isolate.

We pray for improvement in our financial status, our career or relationships. We get overwhelmed on where to start and escape instead. We get caught up in the addictions of choice just to fill the void. Improvements do require one to be open to learning and accepting what could be a flaw no matter your age. It is time to start ruling out opportunities that seem improbable or impossible because someone told you so. If you think it or desire it, it is possible. Experience it and find out! Get out of the "should, ought, must" world and identify what YOU want... not what you think you need. That is thinking in lack. We have millions of needs: getting thin, more money, paying bills, getting enough sleep, eating, hydrating, doing laundry, cleaning... it never ends and most is necessary to live day to day. It is the "want" in between, and the *how to get*, that we fall short and stress about.

Do not be afraid to dream! Remove guilt or shame about those dreams because others give their contradicting input. Who is living your life? I know it seems difficult when you feel cornered by conflicting outside circumstances, but there is always a solution that fits what you want if you look for it and feel you deserve it. You have to make the decision to identify the "what" specifically and sometimes the choice can be initially awkward. It is your responsibility and only yours to make the choice. Remove the voices of others and listen to yourself while in silence. Ask yourself and listen from your heart.

Quietly making excuses for not making decisions anchor those future self judgments into the subconscious and increase the poor attitudes you have about life. Repressing these hidden beliefs further and consistently into your subconscious will cause an explosion one day in any number of dysfunctional ways and yet you can't put your finger on where these negative thoughts are even coming. Your own judgments of yourself hide inside weighing your own self esteem down. You justify that your judgment only applies to others, not to yourself. Easier said than done! How do you feel about you again?

Excuses always seem valid at the time, but it is actually doubt that sneaks in and diverts your direction. So, we give the doubtful thoughts power and accept them as legitimate. This is actually connected to your self esteem as is most things☺. Your worries and concerns cause doubt and your level of esteem can make it worse. Again, a never-ending cycle if we let it.

The excuse made can certainly help you avoid things, but it will decrease your confidence and esteem because you know the real truth if you stop and think about it honestly which we do not do. Excuses are created to make you feel relief about not taking a chance or doing something uncertain. That relief turns into guilt and then fear creeps in behind these excuses. If you are honest with yourself, you continue making excuses with additional layers of reasons why you can't take action now. This keeps your self-esteem level low.

The truth is these excuses only justify taking no action which in turn means no chances or risks are ever involved. You feel relief, but you'll soon realize you are stuck. The excuses limit and hold you back and eventually it is not long before you start to feel bad and worthless. If you constantly avoid taking action then low self esteem amplifies in your mind. Stop saying "I will"! Do you see how this sabotages our magic? We certainly know how to make things disappear. Let us reverse this and start manifesting!

CHAPTER 2

Taking Responsibility

You are your own best friend, so treat
others as you want to be treated
and... start with yourself first...JS

We get frightened at times and begin to doubt ourselves which leads to our need for reassurance from others. You can actually rely on yourself to make things happen, but we have been taught to use others, be like others, confide in others and / or follow others. This opens us up to their opinions again. We are subliminally affected by any negativity and the naysayers who have been living life through rose colored glasses are probably looking through the same glasses of those before them. Maybe the glasses have been soiled for so long, the view has become too annoying to see clearly and one becomes aggravated, abusive or opinionated not realizing they just need to clean the glasses. Your forefathers

hand the dirty glasses to you and you think it is normal to look through dirty glasses. Again, you are
loyal and trusting that someone would not hand
you something that is not perfect to help you see
well.

We can easily get stuck in the past that include pre-
decessors experience and emotion that equate as
regret, remorse, guilt or grief. We have all been
there. This can create a personality that stays in
the past and fearful of moving on experientially
with new thoughts and new experiences. Afraid
of change you say? I reiterate NEW. If you keep
muddling around in the old "should, ought and
must" world, you will stay in that world. If you automatically accept the past direction of your peers
as the whole truth for you, then you fight looking
forward for yourself.

Take note of your pain, but do not dwell on your
lack of or dissatisfaction with life from sorrow.
Identify where the heartache is coming from and
decide if it was even your heartache at all. Did
you inherit it? Dwell on your longing for things.
Write down what these are and stay away from the
self-sabotaging comments I mentioned earlier...
"This is not possible". Your longings will guide

you. If you hear yourself making these sabotaging comments…stop! Give yourself the permission to make the changes. If it isn't working, why keep it the way it is…fix it or get rid of it.

The negativity in the world is exhausting us and I am not excluded from this. For some it is eating away to the point of physical death or at the least a dying soul. It is a daily battle to stay on your own path. The majorities of people live in some degree of fear, uncertainty, want, chaos, lack, or are feeling inadequate and inferior. We don't take the risk or trust that we have what it takes to make the changes. We go back to the external fixations of changing partners, divorce, abandoning children, hop jobs, pop pills or complain about everyone and everything which ultimately can destroy communication with all individuals / countries. We are creating our own chaos! We have lost the ability to dream our own dreams. The magic is gone!

We can trace most every wrongdoing to low self-esteem. We are persistently challenged with the deep question of how to handle the damaging influences residing in and around us. We all have a degree of dysfunction to overcome with experiences of "good and bad", and that is our ultimate purpose. Our purpose is to overcome these obstacles and release the goal for "things" as primary and place them in position that is secondary.

Those people who claim to have our best interests at heart are revealing their own uncertainty when they tear you down. You want more and more "things" to prove them wrong and fill the empty abyss in you. You want what they have...You are letting them be responsible for your feel good. Controlling someone instead of lifting them up shows one feels threatened. Jealousy launches manipulation and fear that one does not feel good enough. This also applies to those who say things to you in a "joking manner" that actually creates quite a 'sting' inside you.

We may regret our actions at times, but we do not need to be weighed down by them. We are expected to make mistakes and without them there is no awakening of the Self. You have to get lost before you find your way and if someone re-directs you, it is always your choice to follow their advice. Taking responsibility for your decision falls on you and you alone. In chapter 28 of "The Many Faces of Self Esteem", I have exercises that will assist you in learning to trust your decisions.

We create our own reality by the amount of responsibility we take for our decisions. I have mentioned this before…but look around at your house and see what the condition is like. How much responsibility have you made to keep it clean and organized? This is also valid for the people we associate with and yet we accept what is there because it is just there. It fills a void. This also works with opposites as well. A rigidly cleaned house can mean you are too inflexible in life. Think about where you are with your decisions and who you keep your company.

Changing yourself doesn't necessarily mean humankind instinctively changes around us. The world can still appear the same as it ever was yet we begin to feel differently toward it. We feel a detachment from the chaos. We begin to see that perfection is there, we just have to notice it. What others do is not your problem, but their problem. Even if what they do affects you directly, you can only change what you are doing and thinking, *not them.*

Standing up for yourself will feel awkward. Feeling awkward signifies you are at the edge of your comfort zone bordering explosion in one direction or the other! Although it will probably be unnerving at first to finally make something happen, it doesn't mean you cannot do it or are not confident enough if you fall back. You may only have so much energy to give in the beginning, so take small steps. Once your energy is gone by giving to others that are needy or taking from others in an equal fashion, it starts costing you your self-esteem and makes it more difficult to pull yourself up again.

People have a tendency to put themselves down and are harder on themselves than anyone else could ever be...and yet if we see something in someone we don't like, we have no problem labeling them as stupid, lazy or irresponsible. This judging only hurts *your* self esteem. The connection is those unfair and rigid rules for others mirrors back at us using the same harsh treatment.

The belief seems to be we can divide our judgments into different groupings. We judge other people by one set of values and judge ourselves by another. This is actually naive. You can't divide your beliefs consciously and keep it all straight. We become experts at justifying why it is appropriate to judge other people harshly and spare ourselves from the same unfair judgment. And yet we sit on our duffs coming up with why we can't have or don't have...

and kick ourselves around the block. It was our choice! I understand we still have a difficult time understanding how we make choices that get results we don't want. The key is you are not growing so you keep making decisions based on old knowledge and possibly even ancient knowledge. It is time to choose to be different! If you are making excuses that you have been dealt a bad hand...the hand you have been dealt is your blueprint, your puzzle to solve.

CHAPTER 3

Whose Choice Is It?

Do not betray yourself...JS

S uffering and illness comes exclusively from our own destructiveness, negativity or unkindness. These are actually areas of our Self that are merely undeveloped areas or blind spots in need of growth. The worry will work on the weakest part of your body and eventually strangle that part causing physical illness. Others may do things to us, but we allow it. We allow it because it simply may be we know no better. Remember that previous saying..."Don't worry yourself sick". You are in debt because you over spend; you are put upon because you allow it. These are choices you have made because you might be afraid of losing "something" or being rejected by someone and in reality that fear is actually causing you to become ill.

It is difficult to accept we have choices in every scenario and yet we listen to others and choose to follow their advice instead of our own; ultimately, kicking ourselves down the road. People become anxious about an uncovered perceived deficiency of "not knowing" an answer for fear that others will realize a flaw in us. We inadvertently want validation from them by accepting their advice. Any thoughts of humiliation, depression or fear from ignoring their judgment keep us from ever feeling "free". We create that which we fret about. It becomes part of you. Change your thinking... change yourself. In my 1st book, "The Many Faces of Self Esteem", I have included exercises that utilize your physical reaction for making comfortable decisions and aiding you in a more correct direction. Practice with these techniques will ferret out the implications put upon you by others.

A negative reaction to an occurrence is a clue of your resistance toward something you probably need to release or change. This reaction may have been learned by acting out or watching someone else act out that received a mixed message of validation. When the expected validation is no longer working we resist. Possibly the learned response comes from a past experience that triggers a similar behavior which resurfaces out of habit. It may be something / someone you know is not for you and yet validation pushes you to get involved and you fold to be accepted. If you continuously experience an intense emotion first-hand and don't like this emotion, you may resist the implication of repeating it which causes anxiety in yourself. This means your own belief about that action or lack of action hasn't been completely resolved in your mind and your body will physically tense up into protection mode. You can even feel your face grimace. Pay attention to those body signals!

When we maintain a jumbled identification with ourselves, we become confused at a crucial time when a wise decision needs to be made. We are not confident at the time so we choke and fold. It is the cause of all confusion. Confusion is telling you to stop until you are sure again. If someone pushes you to make a decision when you are not ready or in a confused state, you can choose to say or think "If I have to make a decision now then my answer is no" or you can say "I have nothing to lose on this and I will follow my gut". The key on the last comment of "having nothing to lose"…make sure this is true. If you really are in a position that will not affect any part of your or others' lives other than a simple risk of "why not", then why not? Learn from it. If it costs you money you can't afford to lose...then do not do it! There are many scam artists out there and they are quite convincing, so you need to be grounded in your own beliefs to protect yourself emotionally and financially! It is your choice in the end but it can be confusing!

"Fusion" is the blending of two or more things and "Con" is in opposition...put together... two or more things are in opposition or disagreement. The 'two or more things' is usually a battle finding yourself and a battle with others trying to find it for you. The mental picture we have of ourselves can be damaged through excessive criticism, no support or encouragement, perceived failure or emotional and verbal abuse. The result is a *confused* low self-esteem level. The above factors including self-centeredness, selfishness, cruelty, vanity, hate and rage can become a part of us to survive, but they are really NOT us.

We were not born with negative behaviors but they are all around us to learn and absorb. We can have high self-esteem at one point and because of broken relationships, divorce, and betrayals we judge our Self and our ability to pick'em right as failure because we should have seen it coming. It isn't always about us! Sometimes it is them and their mask has become so refined they have hooked you emotionally and then financially before you saw the pattern. It exists so learn to fuse the positive with the negative by accepting that both occur, feed both compassion and learn from it so you may become your own pearl...alas, the name of my second book, *Obtaining the Pearl.*

Count how many times a day someone tells you how to do something or what to do? How do you feel every time this occurs? It may be how it was said or what you felt was implied. Again, how it is perceived will identify and affect how you feel! A low self-esteem can cause wild perceptions! You become more confused and agitated and burned out. It may be simply that you need to retreat for a battery re-charge to see things more clearly. If you let all negativity compound itself into your system you may not be able to get out of bed one day. Learning to deflect any internal or external pessimism by creating a healthy release valve that works for you will work on raising your self-esteem level and put you into a better position of identifying what YOU desire to manifest. As you become stronger in your belief systems and more in control of your emotional blowouts, confusion lessens and your choice is more directed.

Life can be a continuous conflict with confusion and fear and it seems when you least need it to materialize. We struggle against any issues that feel depressing, disagreeable, or demanding because there is so much of it. We become overwhelmed and begin to deny our confusion because we get 'stuck in the muck' of thinking we can't change anything therefore it is easier to escape. Stagnation only solidifies the problem even more and initiates new problems. We identified already that resistance, aka confusion, means something needs to change. Many of you feel a lot of struggle and resistance in your life and complain things do not flow easily. And yet I have also seen where things flow easily to people and yet they sabotage it over and over so success stays out of reach. The end result is the same.

Give up the resistance within yourself (your confusion) and the idea you have to struggle to get what you want. Struggle and effort are two different things. New thinking now...we are so tied up with the notion of growth meaning pain that you actually think you are doing good work when you are suffering and working hard. Again we become confused and give up. Focus on what feels right, not so much the results. I have had plans in my head since a kid on where I thought I wanted to be in life and I can honestly say I haven't achieved any of them. I may have even forgot what those plans were...I had been most definitely confused. I couldn't possibly have planned my life to date, where I would live or who I would encounter. I look back and barely remember how I got here. Somehow, I surged through it and yet for many years, I resisted "the flow" causing lethargy and dispassionate goals. I am where I am supposed to be now despite myself and the opinions of others☺ with faith in that higher power of mine and I guess being very stubborn that I would find my way!

Resistance to change is normal and we will feel uncomfortable at first until we realign with the changes. We can misinterpret this awkwardness as *not in our best interest* and value judge the heck out of the change and the people making the changes. Maybe it is to our benefit and maybe it isn't in your best interests. Time will tell but our attitude toward change is the key to successful change. The common source for this resistance is fear of course. These fears are usually related to loss. All change involves letting go at some level and this isn't always easy. We get comfortable being uncomfortable. Real resistance may occur because uncertainties and questions have not been adequately answered.

We don't ask or get clarification because fear of loss, so the unknown end results become scary. When people are frightened, they lash out and judge. Most people live day to day and don't have a future goal or plan B ever in place, so change threatens their whole concept of life as they know it. Changing your attitude about the modification and flowing with it will actually secure your position for the present. If the change doesn't suit you in the end...make your own plans for change.

Much of our unhappiness comes from wanting something one way on the inside and yet accepting less for fear of losing the thing we presently despise. Does this make sense? An example might be we allow someone to dictate our direction or we keep a job that is unfulfilling because we feel helpless to make changes. We feel we have no money or ability to create what we really desire, so we continue to remain unhappy. We allow that inconsistent vibration to resonate at frequencies that eventually manifest losing all of it and now you have nothing.

The higher the self-esteem the closer the belief and actions coincide in favor of your achievements. We act on our belief.

If you are setting goals by what you feel you should be doing according to others' standards rather than what you truly want to do, you are keeping your self-esteem level in limbo and possibly settling or accepting less. Sometimes, we need to follow a direction we may not be sure of, but it may satisfy a need to start somewhere. This gets the energy moving rather than sitting stagnate and complaining. That decision, good or bad, may lead you closer to where you want to be. If you sit and do nothing, nothing will get done. Remember, you are where you are supposed to be at this moment! Without movement of any kind, you will not experience and categorize your "wants and want not" list.

Feelings, not thinking, are part of your intuition that is to be followed. The time has come to listen to your intuition. I had a feeling I needed to move to Cincinnati, a feeling to move to Vegas, a feeling to move to San Diego. I had no idea what was in store for me. When I look back, I followed my feelings but I resisted my decisions internally because I listened to others on why my decisions were poor. I lived in confusion for quite a bit. I hit more walls than anyone can count. I somehow did it my way despite all of the obstacles that reared up in front of me. Yes, I am stubborn, but that saved me.

I tried their way, hitting wall after wall, until it forced me to follow my own feelings. I processed their way apparently wasn't working for me. My stubbornness directed me to refuse ever back tracking or giving up. The only thought I felt and knew was valid for me was to put distance between myself and "their voices" until I figured it out. I knew I wanted something different even though I did not know what "that" was going to be. Alas, the journey begins! The unknown now becomes the adventure! You need to choose if the unknown is your friend or foe. If confusion is holding you back…dive into something you feel you always wanted to try because you are now refining your ability to define friend or foe for yourself and eliminating confusion.

Try it your way. *Follow your hunches and make the choice to follow yourself. Do not allow others to make the choice for you.*

CHAPTER 4

The Unknown - Friend Or Foe?

*It is safe to follow your heart's desire
...deep down you know what to do. JS*

What happens when you meet a new person? You are on a first date or a new job interview and you reason your way through what is real or what their true agenda might be. You don't ask questions because maybe you are desperate and will take anything or you did not research any part further than your nose because you figured you would wing it. You don't even ask yourself if this is a good fit for you. Do I like the location or does it have enough parking? Is the neighborhood respectable so I feel safe? What is the history of someone's family? Everything I talk about points to self-esteem. Do you care enough to know or ask before you enmesh yourself so deeply you can't get loose without feeling great agony? Then you blame the job, your boss or others when things go wrong?

What chances do you take that the person / company you are dealing with have esteem worthy of allowing them into your comfort zone and level of approval? Some are obvious and there are those not so obvious. We allow ourselves to get enmeshed sometimes before we take the time to see if who they say they are and their words follow with coinciding actions. Our hopes are more valid when we know where we stop and someone else begins. If your peace of mind is going to be affected by allowing a person or company to infringe on the value of yourself, more investigation may be needed before a final decision is made.

If you are able to accept the worst possible scenario with what you see, you have created value in your decision. If you are insecure, you will continue to envision the worst and it will show in your behavior or work. It can escalate into more negative visions and snowball into getting fired or having someone break up with you. These values can change depending on how you feel and whom you are with at the time. You are what you accept. If it is learned behavior that even temporarily changes your values or beliefs, it can be changed back if you need. So, there is hope☺ It rests in your hands.

Handling the unknown can and does effect the self-esteem level. If one never takes a chance to try anything new...you begin to feel inadequate, unsure, scared. We all know how it feels to try something new with doubtful anticipation of what is on the other end. Once we make the attempt, we start feeling a drive that wasn't there before and the more you are comfortable continuing it; hence, the more comfortable you are in taking chances in the future. Even if the outcome is not good, you now know it is not something you want in your life again. Check that one off the list! You are conquering your fear of the unknown and gaining answers about yourself that helps refine and define who you are becoming.

Fear is not meant to be a fiend that terrorizes or paralyzes you. It may unsettle you but fear is there to make you aware of what is blocking your progress. We know fear can exasperate us to do things or say things we may not say under calmer circumstances. We all react differently to the unknown. Some people avoid change by never changing, some panic which makes them feel out of control, some are curious and ponder the unknown cautiously and there are those that look at the mysterious head on. The unknown is a doorway to something new. The answer to fear is never think beyond the present. It is to think less and have faith in the flow of life. It is to release instead of grabbing to hold on. It is not alright to sacrifice your integrity just to fit in or accept less. Do you stay in your comfort zone of lack to feel safe? It will always be scary to make the change, but change your attitude that your heart will guide you appropriately. Every scenario is a two way street and you need to evaluate the part you have played in the scene. Change does not need to be so overwhelming that we avoid the developmental journey altogether. Refine the parts you can see or don't like. Experience more to see those blind spots or if you are really brave, ask someone you admire and trust what they perceive.

Going back to entering a new relationship; we may see red flags, but because it is new we ignore or assume the flags will go away as the relationship continues. We have all been there and done that! You become more familiar and comfortable with each other and now the red flags get buried in what appears to be the good parts. Those red flags revert to being an unknown until they reappear more magnified later! We get confused because accepting flaws is part of what we were taught. Clue…The red flags are actually a precursor to things that are going to become way more amplified in the future! No one told us that! Yes, we all have things to overcome, but red flags are an opportunity to really take a look and see if we can accept the person because we know we can't change them. If you can accept all aspects up front, you have chosen that life and yes, you created it!

If someone appears to be the stronger or more stable of the two, the stronger may unknowingly encourage the neediness for attention, love and support from the weaker of the relationship by enabling "needs" which have been "fine-tuned" over the years. You appease them, buy them things, build them up, and cater to them until you realize their neediness grows with increased giving. One's frustration starts to ignite and hence begins the feeling of inadequacy of the stronger by providing more and more what the partner needs which really is a never-ending bottomless pit you cannot fill. You are not going to win that battle. There was a flag, but we overlooked it as needing to love and nurture "the flag" with hope that our giving would melt their needs away.

Stay on track with your intentions no matter what is going on. The predator will insist they have no power to change anything and that even if they tried, nothing changed. Those that present the evidence that nothing is changing and matters are simply getting worse and worse are those who still doubt themselves and let others handle their every move. When one is challenged by dishonest intentions and one is asked to deviate from their path, one must look at the consequences of complying. Feeding into their manipulation may be an indicator of chronic low self-esteem in you. To stand up for what you believe to stay focused is paramount, but you must know what you truly believe. Making excuses, putting it off or being apologetic for one's belief or lack of belief is not acceptable. It is a time of responsibility for both now to stand strong, firm and produce for themselves. We are no one's keeper.

We have talked about boundaries in my other books, and without them we become unsafe with ourselves. We can become depressed, drained, shut off, less social and depending on our way of handling these unknown dragons in front of us will be the way we progress with any situation. Without boundaries, life never seems to change for the better. You want to escape but someone's neediness or self-sabotaging behavior has a hold on you. You may feel it is a duty or responsibility to follow through with the obvious wrong choice made by "the unknown" factors from the start. Again the loyalty issue has surfaced or you still feel you can fix the other person. It is now expected that you give until it hurts and believe me it will either financially or emotionally. What made the giver feel good in the beginning is now taken for granted. The "taker" assumes the well is always full to take anything desired! No matter what it does to you!

How do we identify the unknown parasites ready to pounce on us? It is a risk to trust. Sometimes we don't know until a pattern develops over time. Parasitic "taking" can be activated with excessive giving to someone. They found a giver! Sure, they will follow you! You give because you are attracted to someone and want to impress or make their life easier. It may also be your way to hook into that personality trait that masked as positive attention you crave. Maybe they were poor growing up and you want to provide what they didn't have to make them feel good. Wow, isn't that a nice feeling? They seem to like it and appear to appreciate it! Be aware that it can be usual for someone who had to survive without boundaries to learn to mooch. Again, what is your need that you overlook sincere appreciation vs. a skewed way of life? What are the historical facts of their life and present end result to show for where they are in life? They can certainly justify the problems they have incurred. It is always a good story and usually heart wrenching to a giver.

You think 'maybe I need to keep giving because they just aren't quite on their feet yet. It must be hard for them!' You want to give more because there is an instant (although) temporary pleasure for you. If they never say thank you or start expecting you will save them, you may even convince yourself they just don't know how to show their appreciation because they never had "things" before. Then you find out, they give to someone else to impress them. Ho Hum. You worked hard for the money and their gratitude is to give it away or never use it. They become bored again and again. You keep trying to make it right. In the end you are beating a dead horse. This is not love. They become mean or start blaming you for the relationship going wrong. "If you would have done

this……". "I will find someone who does care"…..
If you sit there shaking your head in disbelief that
this is happening, don't fret…it is exactly as you
see it.

They are parasites that have drained you of all and
when you finally strangle their supply of *whatever*,
they will move on but not without making you feel
guilty and less than as a person. Actually, you have
done it to yourself by letting it go on so long, but
we have all been there at least once in our lives and
maybe more hoping we will learn our lesson next
time. It never goes away until we have learned our
lesson.

So if you keep getting what you get, maybe take a
closer look at you, not them. These unknown patterns, whether ours or theirs, can be devastating
because we didn't take the time to evaluate or ask
questions in the beginning. Love is blind and usually the so called unknowns were the red flags you
buried. If you continuously do not assess these flags
in the beginning, their contradicting actions relat-
ing to your true values and beliefs become a lifestyle
that causes you to retreat away from future inspirations. We become loners with a fairly high wall to
get over.

Looking back in time, people with chronically low self-esteem usually have been neglected or abused in some way as a child. They feel a lot of hidden anger and anxiety about not feeling worthy. This spills over into feeling like a victim of circumstance and certainly less than a good emotional situation can make them very sensitive to feeling abandoned or rejected again. They kick into survival mode. They constantly "run with a dark cloud above them". They learn to be manipulative, lie, and sneak to meet their needs and those that felt sorry for this neglect are the ones that usually end up giving with no boundaries to appease the child's fear of rejection. The child starts to realize that being the victim can reap rewards! And so it goes into adulthood. What is yours is mine and what is mine is mine. Feel sorry for me more and more please... How could you have known all this or avoided it?

As this child *now predator* gets older, the price tag can get more expensive for the giver. The predator now has to create trust and has learned to wear the mask of "having" to lure in the giver who has what they need to survive another round of "not having". They say all the right things, agree with all your past emotional injuries and just make you feel "they get you". Your soul mate has arrived finally! Once the predator knows they "have you", they begin to start chipping away at this beautiful relationship you thought you found. Again, how could you have avoided this?

They start censoring your thoughts and feelings, everything becomes your fault and they start to criticize when there used to be compliments. They control where you go or question where you have been, they love one minute but angry the next and your feelings don't count because it really is all about their survival! You begin to question your own sanity as they never seem to remember promising you anything and they have sent mixed messages to keep you on their path. They make the rules as they go to meet their ever-changing agenda. When things go wrong, they blame you and anyone else they can think of without a blink of an eye. Friend or foe is the bloody unknown now. How did we miss all this? We are smart and kind and caring! Who would do this? They didn't need to do all this, we would have loved them!

This is the ultimate behavior of someone void of esteem. How did you not see it coming? The only thing I can say is one needs to really pay attention, take time before you give it all away just to have someone, and if it doesn't feel right or too good to be true…it isn't. They are usually transparent all in good time if you wait and they will usually have a myriad of addictions that surface because they live recklessly. They drink, drink and drive, gamble, have multiple ego boosters running at the same time (companionships or as they say…*just friends*). A healthy relationship survives only when there is balance between what is given and what is taken from the relationship no matter what type of relationship.

Please don't beat yourself up if you find yourself at the end of this disaster or in it. It will not be easy to escape unless you become strong again and this is not easy as they have been beating you down possibly for years. Find a support system you trust and feel safe. You are already feeling wrath from yourself, so you don't need others telling you what you did wrong. Now you are back into the unknown… feeling inadequate and confused. What you thought you knew becomes foreign to you. Hopefully, in time, after multiple beatings in the heart chakra you learn to be a friend to yourself first. It is so necessary to allow a healthy amount of time in solace to heal effectively. You certainly do not want to repeat this again. You will become your own foe if you do not take note of your own dysfunctional patterns and correct them.

Relationships are a prime example of an unknown. They can be the worst unknown because emotions get involved too quickly where trying something new like hot air balloon rides is easier to check off your list if you don't like it. So, journeying into your own unknown to better your understanding of who you are will actually strengthen your ability to see others as friend or foe. Take your time, find your joy and set a boundary realizing the new world is beckoning for everyone to be responsible for themselves. Give and take needs to be equal or as close to it as one can get. I am not saying dollar for dollar…but if true and honest emotional support and caring is important, what is it worth to you?

Accept the balance that makes both happy. If it becomes a condescending or demeaning end result to someone, someone is stuck and needs to re-evaluate. Again, this is a choice. Are you going to accept being stuck? Everyone comes into our life for a reason. See the gift of the lesson if it comes from a silver lining of loss or an unexpected separation. Feed compassion to the lesson, bless it on its way out and say it is their karma to deal with, not mine.

CHAPTER 5
Are You Stuck?

Allow yourself to feel Freedom
and Power....JS

We become sad because we become stuck in the past. When you get stuck in thoughts of limitation or continue to self-sabotage your success, you sink into the illusion of believing it because you have picked up thoughts from someone else or no one ever pushed you past those fears of failing when you were young. You have become "bound" to certain realms of experience which came from "a lack of" in the past or someone else's lack that became inherent to you. Becoming "unbound" or unstuck often advances along a process we now relate to as inner growth. You are slowly transforming yourself with every experience whether you realize it or not. If you believe "you are already perfect"... you are actually bouncing back into your original

JOANNE SALSBURY

state of what already exists. We have been taught that we have to earn this state of perfection again and if we fall short we did something wrong thereby being imperfect.

Understand that "perfect" does not mean that learning is over and you are flawless. It means you accept all aspects of yourself, good and bad and you have a sense of satisfaction for life relative to your already pure essence. What or whence came those chains that have bound progress to ever feeling satisfied or content with what we choose?

Everyone grieves from external issues such as divorce, death, disease, bankruptcy etc. at some point in our lives. Anything can distress us if we allow it and can cause a severe setback emotionally or financially. If you resist the bad by putting your head in the sand or closing down, you are adding another layer of insecurity that keeps you from flowing freely. It is another layer to get tangled in. This creates that riptide of confusion which leads us back to sadness or depression. We lose our inspiration and passion. You go deeper and deeper into the abyss of feeling stuck.

Believe it or not, you are here to nurture yourself first. This is hard to swallow for most all of us! We were taught / told to: work hard, give to others, just get a paycheck, just do anything because everyone is struggling in these days of lack... get with the program, it is not worth getting if you don't work hard for it, give till it hurts, fight to survive, you cannot trust anyone, fend for yourself at any one's expense, it is them or you. People are trying to follow these rules when they are already confused.

These opinions cultivate life as a struggle and that suffering is necessary to have anything and people are getting tired. Yes, this is all true if you are giving your "all" from a level of lack in your own life. You do need to make an effort and pay the bills and you do need to keep moving forward to live. The struggle comes because you are following a road that goes where and who told you to take that road?

We want to surrender and trust our intuition, but the fear of rejection, failure or letting go of things control, block and freeze us up. It is difficult to overcome the old habitual thinking of struggling and fighting for everything. The most difficult concept for us is to "be" and not "do". I was humbled with the saying of "Be, Know and then Do" in that order. I could not grasp the order. We are conditioned if we don't do…we don't know…therefore we can't "be" what we want to be. It would even appear in my first chapters that this is what I am saying. But what I did not make stand out was being specific about what you want to Be or have first. If you are wishy washy about your goals, you keep *doing* in hopes that the *doing* leads you to the Being. This could take forever with many hit and misses. This is not wrong, but will take longer and cause the struggles we are feeling. Unfortunately most of us have been following this method. We also know there are others who "just knew" what they wanted to Be and when they achieved it, it would seem to us as being blessed or dealt the right hand. They knew what to BE, they gained the Know and started Doing.

If you think struggling to "Do" by giving and working for the good of others first will absolve you from being lost, you are mistaken. I see people who give and do for others saying that "all will come from God" and the good life will be repaid eventually. They guilt you into putting other's first even though you give from an empty well whether it is emotional or financial. The more responsibility you shoulder for their needs while paying no attention to your own needs actually create more struggles for you and could put you into an early grave. You become numb and lose sight of your own humanness. Now you become frustrated, overburdened and feel empty because you keep on contributing from an empty, confused vessel that had little to give from initially and worry now rears its ugly head for your own self.

Fears takes worry's place, but remember that fear is precursor for something that needs to change. Obviously, something is out of balance. To balance, you need to get that flow of living in which YOU feel inspired and joyful by what you do without feeling the pressure to do it. Pressure signals that you are not free and that you are attached to the end result. If you feel pressure to produce for others because they keep asking or taking and you need validation...oops, you might be surprised at the end result. The saying "Love yourself before you can love others" means just this. If you are not whole, you will sink at the slightest bit of turbulence. God is not asking this of you. God wants everyone to be happy and feel loved.

Fear is necessary to initiate change if we allow it; otherwise we may never experience new things in life. Fear marks the boundaries between what feels safe and familiar to you and what doesn't (the unknown) which we have discussed. Beyond that frontier there is something new which you do not understand or have not yet experienced. We yearn to explore the new when our self-esteem is strong or getting there. On the other side of fear is experience. Fear is a clue to those things you have closed down. Are you a worrier? How often does that worry imprison you and / or makes you stop experiencing? Worry and fear closes the star gate to a higher form of you. If you feel that worry is out of control, let go and jump through!

The worry wants to flow through you and if you flow with it, it will bring you to another reality. This is where you want to be. You sabotage yourself by making comments like "What am I doing wrong, everything I do doesn't work, why am I so lost..." This is mind babble from past comments you may have heard from others or you get so set on one path that may not be the best for you. If you keep hitting a wall over and over, maybe it is time to look for another door.

It feels so degrading to be afraid to say or do anything because of how someone else will react. Being controlled is when someone limits our freedom emotionally or physically or influences us into doing something we don't want to do. We allow it which keeps us stuck. We are afraid of losing what is perceived as security of the situation when in fact, it may not be secure at all. They control that as well.

The same is true with work goals, money or relationships. If you doubt that you will have success, and let others control your direction it is a sign that you need work on your self-esteem. Poor self-esteem will keep you stuck and cause you to become negative before you even get started. You become jealous and rooted in the fear that you do not have value and that others are more rewarded than you because you are always comparing yourself. It isn't what you think others have, it is what you think you don't have…you are stuck in your own thinking. You achieve to impress which will get you nowhere in the end.

Your thoughts are so powerful! Start making a list when one of those limiting thoughts come into your head or say it into a recorder. List your actual desires and then write next to it what your fear is in relation to this desire. Those thoughts unparalleled with the desire are keeping you stuck. You have to practice being positive. We are so ladened with negativity from the news and people, in general, who are in same boat, it is very difficult to even know what reality is for us. I was taught for every 1 minute of negative input into our system takes 10 minutes of positive to wipe it out. Get busy or you will drown in the negative.

Check yourself when you are being negative or confronting others. Use this to break through old beliefs. It takes courage to stop attacking the source of "different information and opinion" and to look in the mirror and see what lies beyond the mirror. Yes, we are perfect, but not flawless. We still need builders to assist us in the process of building and everyone is skilled at something different. The negative enforcement is just as powerful a builder as the positive re-enforcement! Do not use negativity as your excuse for not accomplishing.

We have a tendency to transfer underlying feelings, needs, expectations and beliefs from childhood or former relationships onto people in our lives. It usually ends up being the ones closest to us. When the past surfaces unknowingly, we might expect to slip back into old behaviors or familiar responses to old situations without realizing it. Obviously, identifying this baggage and placing it in the "no longer me" file would be growth for everyone!

Being "stuck" and continuing to think poorly about yourself will make finding solutions much harder. Not allowing yourself to try new things and challenge yourself can be sources of anxiety and major frustration. You will have a low tolerance and give up easily always waiting for someone else to take over and rescue you. Temporary setbacks will seem permanent. Remember when your parents rescued you instead of teaching you to get through it…it becomes a habit to let others do the same.

People become petrified of facing the emptiness of not knowing why they are stuck. They seek out external means to cope. They need acknowledgement, admiration, power, and attention all of the time and I mean all of the time! If they don't get it, they fall into depression and hopelessness or become desperate. So in retrospect, when you praise your children to build them up for no reason, it is having an opposite effect. Teach them to applaud themselves, to feel good about what they do right by asking how they feel about what they did. If they did something wrong or inappropriate, use the same process. Ask them how they feel about the poor choice they made. Your praise or compliment to them comes from their identifying their own validation of what they did and confirming that aspect. Example: When they bring you a picture they drew (it could be unrecognizable)…ask them what it represents and how they feel about what they drew…would they do anything differently …do they like what they drew…whatever their answer…validate that answer and thank them for the gift of the picture.

You don't want them to be afraid of being rejected by saying what a horrible drawing and yet you don't want to create a need for constant re-affirming for no reason (*constant re-affirming by others usually will not occur when one becomes an adult*.) If the value comes from them, it teaches them to evaluate themselves without fear. As children age they become stuck needing this constant validation if you have overly praised them as a child and they can become quite hypersensitive. You will recognize them at work because they complain no one tells them they are doing a good job. You know if you are doing a good job or not and the validation needs to come from inside of you. Realize you are showing your colors to the world by the words that come out of your mouth.

CHAPTER 6

Do As I Say, Not As I Do...

Example is not the main thing
in influencing others,..
...it is the only thing... Albert Schweitzer

Over the years, we hear and see ideas / images from our parents, family, peers, school, etc which develop our opinions and beliefs about ourselves during our childhood. We start to role play without even knowing we are doing it and alas, we develop a personality: a set of habits, behaviors, and beliefs that forecast future thoughts or decisions! Our personality is based on combined lineage prevalent to our history and experience. Do they belong to us or are they traditionally passed down to us?

We are that empty computer waiting to be programmed to function in this world. We are handed "the personality", but we are not taught to process or weigh these opinions and beliefs for ourselves to see if it fits our pre-destined mold. As you innocently grow and experience, you begin to get tongue lashings, finger waving, or the tried and untrue of value judging which backhands the whole idea of becoming an individual snowflake. In my first book, The Many Faces of Self Esteem, I go into more depth about all this and how it gets by us to the point we want to find an escape from ourselves which is not the goal.

Due to these influences acquired in youth, we can be held back from our own unfolding for a long time. I disclose my own experience of this in my first books. We try to conform to what is demanded of us out of loyalty to our teachings and that adjustment almost always brings discomfort and confusion. Because of our own learned powerlessness, parents and teachers do not often give children faith in themselves and their inner resources. These exterior influences can be very compelling and decisive for us because it becomes our belief and belief molds our decisions. We begin to become defined by the constraints we feel we have to stay within. This is what is causing the frustrations, anger, anxiety and confusions all which can lead to depression and so forth.

If you believe others can influence your life negatively, then so it is…if you believe you cannot be happy until this or that change, then so it is. Whatever 'it' is that you are focusing on whether positive or negative will come into your experience and grow if you keep feeding it the same food. It is difficult to trust ourselves because we keep playing the thoughts or tapes that others have provided for us that keep us limited.

Pay attention to those little "thought zingers" that slip through. Those little devils are so fast we have moved onto the next thought before we can process it. It happens more, I believe, when we get tired or dealing with something so long, you almost are ready to give up. The feelings of insecurity and doubt begin to enter the "zone" of motivation. If your self-esteem is lower than it needs to be at that time, you get stuck in that zone of doubt and it begins to take over. You start to manifest the doubt part which has now become more of the focus.

As a child, we learned that feelings of limitation seemed correct and valid by what we heard and mimicked by our peers of example: be insignificant *as manifested by neglect,* seen and not heard, adjust, *be a good citizen,* be a good parent, be responsible by following "the rules", do not be different, do not think outside the box or you will not be accepted. This is not to say we should have carte blanche on our behavior because respect and trust of each other creates the healthy boundaries to follow and we do need to have a plan to interact with others effectively and still be ourselves. We start to hide or mask the individual side of ourselves that is supposed to be growing into an individual personality of our own.

Will you be an outcast or shunned if you dare to be different and explore the unknown? If you have a focus that you are passionate about and it isn't going to cause harm to yourself or anyone else… you only have yourself to answer. They say Sir Isaac Newton never had sex because his religious belief was no sex before marriage. He was too busy with his math and mental puzzles to bother marrying. Ben Franklin was considered a security risk as he had a "passion for virtue" that made him outspoken on issues that were borderline controversial at the time and required to have 3 body guards so as not to arouse people while he was out. Both followed their passion at the cost of normal human interface. They followed their beliefs. It was their choice with no regrets that we know about anyway.

Our reactions always have to do with our own self judgments and feelings of inadequacy or strength, not the other person. When you feel that emotion erupting from someone's comment, turn your thinking back to yourself and ask yourself what the problem is...when you learn to accept that changes are needed to become a new you, your world will begin to change along with your attitude about how others interact with you or toward you. For example, if someone makes an observation about you and verbalizes it...it may be something you already judge about yourself so it has *sting*. However, if they make the same remark and you don't have that particular judgment about yourself; it probably won't bother you at all. You may even laugh or be able to laugh at yourself.

When an emotion is coming from you like jealousy, it is because you doubt yourself. An example given to me is... if you and a friend are trying to lose weight, you wouldn't feel jealous if your friend hit her mark before you if you are confident you would eventually meet yours as well. You would be happy for her. We have a tendency to gossip or berate others for the very things we are not accomplishing for ourselves. This is not a new fact. So, those who do value judge others are really exposing their own inadequacies. If you are trying to hide from others and from yourself, this is not the way to do it. You are actually waving a red flag.

Doing what I say and not what I do has been long standing and no one is exempt from having said or done it. It is what we have seen and heard for centuries and beyond. We are now developing into a totally different mindset about this issue. Some will remain trapped and continue to judge as they ignore their own shortcomings. They will continue to assume the other person needs "fixed".

The courageous person will see that we do not need to control or judge others as it is wasted and non-productive energy. Your level of self-esteem is key here. Hopefully, people will realize there is no true accomplishment in perfection but satisfaction of having accomplished. If we are all dictating perfection for others, or we accept others' words as true, we will remain depressed, confused and bouncing around like an ant with their antennas cut off. Children act out because they don't know how to respond appropriately. This continues into adulthood if not guided by appropriate example.

CHAPTER 7

Am I Acting Out...?

The possibilities are numerous once
we decide to act and not react
... GEORGE BERNARD SHAW

We act out when we don't know what is really going on inside of us. It is a defense mechanism used most usually without impulse control. We are rarely in a frame of mind at this point to process what we do or how we act. We escalate into a mode of reacting. We are thinking so fast toward finalizing a problem nobody is cognizant if the response is valid, healthy, or self-serving. Everyone is now defending themselves and buttons are pushed. How do we act out? This chapter is going to focus mostly on the signs and actual things we have experienced, seen or heard that creates a self-esteem issue. As I have said in past, in order to make changes, we have to know what to look for and then we can change it. Some ideas I will expound upon are actual data pulled from other sources. No need to re-invent the wheel, but I do feel it is important to be aware.

****These situations always begin with child and parent/ guardian interaction or neglect of interactions, so carrying acting out behavior forward is usual no matter what the age.* Handling new situations is uncomfortable for anyone. We talked about the unknown and how some look forward to the unknown as a challenge and others become paralyzed. Even emotionally paralyzed people can react with fervor. Obviously, everything is new to a child so we need to introduce them to everything we can. I remember I was taught never to touch crystal but those prismatic color qualities fascinated me and still do☺. So what would a child do but wait till everyone is gone and touch it. Murphy's Law states that something usually breaks.

Later in years, a mentor of mine suggested another way to handle the situation. Take the time to let the child hold the crystal in a safe and monitored way in the presence of an adult until the fascination no longer exists as strongly as before. Made sense to me! Take time…this could eliminate behavioral overreactions instead of ignoring the situation by assuming one understands the end result of their inappropriate behavior.

I was rarely taken to the grocery or restaurants when young probably to eliminate any chance of acting out. My parents chose not to put themselves in the position that most every parent has embarrassingly experienced. It would have required my parents to discipline me if I got rambunctious in public (which kids do) and they cared too much what others would think. This did make it difficult for me in social situations later in years and maybe my brothers as well. I was one that became paralyzed because I did not know what to say in public. I was quiet and shy for fear of the consequences☺ which is also a form of acting out.

Yet, we had carte blanche to explore the forest, woods and open areas without direct parental supervision. Looking back, this was where my parents were more comfortable. They felt safe because that is what they were used to growing up. I could act out all I wanted, but didn't need to because I was pleasantly occupied. I still prefer the wide open spaces more than the closed in areas of cities because I was allowed to feel free in that environment. Through education and pushing to learn the set of skills I lacked allows me to feel assured and less paralyzed in public. I know I can handle myself well in any social situation now if I choose. I was thirsty to learn about social skills because I did not like feeling inept and I knew I had better figure it out. Sure I learned etiquette for all of the silent issues like which fork to use and how to walk properly growing up, but if not combined with verbal ability…it scares you the first time around in real life and you act out by freezing up, sitting in a safe corner or clinging to your partner with a death grip.

I do have a pet peeve with parents who actually take time to expose their children to enclosed public areas. I commend you for exposing them, but many let them run wild with no guidance to interact appropriately in that situation. The goal is teach them to behave with the proper etiquette necessary when out in public. If not guided early on, as they get older, they may do damage to properties, deface buildings and bridges, and have an "I don't care about you or your things… attitude". Teaching does take time and effort, and if the balance of learning and practicing is done early on in years (preferable), the following growth years will be less strenuous, less costly and the child will feel more balanced. No acting out necessary.

As an adult, some may be uncomfortable in a new job, new neighborhood or a party where you know no one. Again, if you are confident with yourself you will have no problems, but if you were not trained to flow and experience, you may want to leave as soon as you get there. This is not fun to feel this way. Make this a goal of overcoming what seems to be a debilitating obstacle. I wonder now if my mother had a social anxiety disorder because she would not go out unless with us, yet she was quite talkative in safe situations.

Positive attention is profoundly needed at an early age and feeling neglect lowers the self-worth of a child in later years as not being worthy of anything. The only behavior that got immediate results for any attention was acting out of screaming, yelling, kicking, and temper tantrums which usually worked because the parent gives in to keep them quiet. The child sees this acting out thing works and uses it as a means to gratify. Especially in children, acting out is a cry to actually subdue anger, impatience, dissatisfaction and instant need for gratification. Acting out can be exhausting.

In adults, it is more serious as they become needy and usually drain the life from others because of all the constant attention and validation needed to keep them going. Adults normally grow out of the temper tantrums even though I can't say completely. I have seen adults throw just as big a tantrum as a child. Not a pretty sight and one would think embarrassing. I literally watched a friend have one moment lost in receiving attention from the spouse in military (who was on a submarine) immediately have affairs just for attention. Voids within you exacerbate a drop into wandering eyes, depression, adultery, alcohol/drugs, rash behavior…whatever the choice learned. One also sees "acting out" behaviors when the word "No" is used. A good first clue to beware…

Independence is what we all want. This doesn't mean we want to be alone, but being miserable with someone is worse than being alone with yourself or to some anyway. We start telling children from the time they are born what we want them to do, say or be. We are teaching them for sure, but how are we doing it? Are we telling them what to do or guiding them to make their own decisions? We hope to communicate how to stay out of harm's way and to do what we or the general public expects in principle only. It is not meant to be a programmed horse trail. No wonder there is acting out! I cover this more in *The Many Faces of Self Esteem,* so I won't repeat myself. We strip any hope of teaching independence when we tell them what to do, how to live or where to work and then pay no attention to what their actions are saying.

Many people have excess energy that needs released whether it is mentally or physically and become bored easily if not directed and taught proper productive ways. They fall into addictions and bad habits picked up by others who may have the same issue but were never taught to direct the energy into productive hobbies or sports. Misery loves company. All a form of acting out! Create a healthy outlet for yourself no matter who you are...a hobby. Find what gives you nourishing enjoyment that helps balance your emotions.

The NIMH found in its research that the cause for serious acting out include the following:

- Weak bonding with parents, caused by parents being physically or emotionally unavailable to the child
- Impotent parenting as manifested by failing to watch over children, by being excessively strict, or by providing harsh and inconsistent discipline

- A home environment that exposes children to violence and supports and models aggressive and violent behaviors
- The impact of rejection by or competition with peers in early school years (In some cases this experience results in children who do not succeed socially or academically banding together to act out. This tendency to band together appeared to be true of the Columbine High School perpetrators.)
- Gender (From approximately the age of four years, boys were found by the NIMH study to be more likely than girls to engage in aggressive, acting out behaviors.)
- Child psychopathology (The NIMH study suggests that children with behavioral difficulties are likely to have two or more psychological problems such as conduct or anxiety disorders or depression.)
- Lower socioeconomic status (A correlation between low **family** income and antisocial acting out has been repeatedly noted.)
- Heredity (Perhaps the most surprising factor of the NIMH study has been the possibility that genes may indeed influence behaviors. Exactly how genetics affects personality and mental illness is not clearly understood. How

the environment interacts with this genetic component also remains a mystery. However, in 2004 this genetic ingredient in acting out behaviors was a topic of study for the NIMH.)

- Problems identified for this group of children include the following:
- exhibiting a lower attention span
- being more difficult to comfort
- being more timid and bashful
- showing more aggression and acting out
- doing poorer on academic testing for early skills
- showing a less positive response to being in school
- showing less ability to form positive relationships with other children

Among the forms of acting out behavior seen in children and teens that warrant professional attention are the following: It is more difficult to curtail when they become adults as it becomes part of their MO. The consequences also become more serious as one gets older.

- pathological lying
- bullying others
- self-injury, such as cutting self or head-banging

- alcohol or drug abuse
- truancy
- running away
- participating in unsafe sexual activities
- getting into fights
- assault
- vandalism
- fire-setting
- stealing
- rape
- homicide

I feel this is all noteworthy and as I said there is no reason to reinvent the wheel as NIMH has bulleted it quite nicely I feel. Working in this type environment where I see the end result of the neglect, I can vouch for the validity.

Understand emotions that get out of control are a form of acting out. If anyone can relate to any of these and I think we all can to some degree, we know we need some work. This is ok. There is no need to be embarrassed or hide from it. I am still amazed at some of the history and experience people live through. It is no wonder we react. We will continue to react intensely if we don't learn to understand the why of intensity.

Reacting is ok...emotions are normal to all of us. It is the intensity and reason for the emotion and does it get out of control? People need to work through their natural emotions, but we know that trying to resolve a situation at the highest intensity of the emotion is not effective. Excuse the situation until both people are more calm and rational.

Maybe you need to set limits and provide a consequence that is equal to the infraction (make the consequence equal to the infraction, not punitive but learning). This is much easier if you know where the line is drawn for yourself. If your boundaries are weak, you tend to over re-act or not re-act at all.

Again, the level of your own esteem will dictate the level of acting out. We expect children to over re-act as they are in a learning curve and need guidance. When an adult over re-acts, it is more difficult to resolve and your own boundaries need to be clearer to stick to your guns and follow through. In reality, it is the same for children. If your boundaries are unclear and not verbalized, the children will take over. I see this all of the time in my business. Parents bring their children in to be "fixed". It is clear that the parents need educated first.

Understand if you cannot get your emotions or the emotions of a child under control you may need to get professional help, but please don't assume that only the child needs the help. It is always a two way street. The lack of balance could be more one-sided of course but nevertheless, we can all use reminders or more education to refine our own re-actions. Isn't it much better when we have control and reason with a solution that is win-win?

CHAPTER 8

Living For The Past

What is past is prologue...
WILLIAM SHAKESPEARE

The past shapes us but should not become our crutch to command our present and future. There comes a point in time when we have to take responsibility for anything that occurred in the past whether it was under our control or not. We become so dependent on what was and allow our thoughts to remain in sync with the beliefs created because of the past behaviors and examples of others. If you think it has to be this way, you need to rethink this. At what age can you do this? I suppose the "legal age" is a start but now days they have public assistance for anyone of any age that can offer a helping hand. If you are of age where you can make your own decisions, and the old decisions / thoughts don't feel right to you, change them. I was taught a mantra that

I still use even though much less now…"That was
then, this is now and everything has changed".
When you feel the old outdated tape or vision
come into your thought / vision space…say the
mantra over and over quickly until the tape stops
or the vision goes away. Replace it with what you
want it to be…

People become dependent on living in the past.
"I should have married that person when I had
the chance"… "That *someone* abused me in a manner that damaged me forever"… "I never had
a parent growing up and I am jealous of those
that had guidance" …"We never had money and
they don't understand…they were spoon fed…I
wasn't and therefore I can justify my lack of respect". This list can go on as everyone has some
tale of woe. Can it stop? Who needs to stop it? If
you are waiting on "it" to "happen" for you, you
will be waiting forever. All the medication or self-
medication techniques in the world are not going
to make "it" happen either! Living in the past is
another escape.

Much of our "hurt" comes from a past unresolved
instance that will create a sting when relived. You
may experience relief and hopefully insight that

you were probably not in control of the original occurrence and a victim of the "self-esteem level of the offender". The old insight doesn't have to be part of your "now" as I mentioned before. You can choose to forgive these hurts, accept them as part of you as I mentioned in "Obtaining the Pearl" and understand that you were only doing what you knew to do at the time as were the people involved in the interaction or lack of interaction. Today can be different. Remember, accepting and forgiving does not mean you need to tolerate the same behaviors now or in the future.

Some of the hooks that keep you attached could be peer or parental pressure, expert emotional manipulators that chip away at you and keep you weak (abusers), over-dependency or vulnerability that causes you to stay attached. Some get trapped into unhealthy enabling to resolve another's situation to suppress their own the past. You may have to detach from persons, places or things that are harmful for you and keep you from progressing. People grow apart. Change is inevitable. Take the gift of the lesson and move on. It hurts because you want to have allegiance to the people you felt you had a connection to and we don't like change or letting go of connections.

There are times we let go and fall right into a similar situation that is masked differently because we were so happy to get out of last deal! We pay no attention to the new flags that resemble the past flags. Over time, you will get sick and tired of being "sick and tired". If you do not have new insight, you will become physically or emotionally ill and shut down. That wall becomes too high to get over.

You really have to be careful not to get caught in the quicksand of poor coping, self-pity or illness due to past hurts because you have stuffed the resentment back into your own body over and over only for it to resurface as an intense emotion which eventually become physical ailments. The past can haunt and in reality, you are doing it to yourself if you don't wake up and realize you can change the present and future. The biggest problem I see is many people don't realize they have a problem. We point the fingers when we need to stick the mirror up to our own face. Accusations or excuses are masking the past hurts and an ideal time to identify what we may be holding onto that is so difficult to release. I know, easier said than done.

The past is the past. The people that helped create your path had their own issues that may have transferred to you as a different problem. Sometimes the experiences people shield you from create a whole new set of circumstances for you. It works in opposite for the things they do expose you to that may not be in your best interest. It still comes back to realizing that whatever has occurred in the past can be halted by you, but it will take time with a change of beliefs, thoughts and practice. If you do not think you can do on your own then seek assistance. Do not always rely on family or friends to help as you may not get an objective point of view and you may not feel safe in doing so. You are trying to get rid of baggage and not acquire more by opening the gates of the "should, ought and must" world.

Our purpose isn't to acquire aids to mask hurts from the past, but refine our souls to love all the flaws and imperfections. It may be the irritation that births your pearl. Pearls, as you know, start as an irritation to the mollusk. When you have low self-esteem there is an irritation that has not been nurtured. When your peers / family feel low themselves due to their past circumstances their value transfers to you in multiples daily by default. The nurturing environment is so fierce the pearl may never survive. The more extreme your insecurities, the more chance of becoming paranoid that people hate us, are after us, out to get us or are always talking about us etc.... We can visually see the insecurities in a person who thinks this way by the way they sit or stand, eye contact or no eye contact, isolative and quiet. This dysfunction has created wars!

Once we change our perspective, the world changes with us. We all have a hidden hurt that inhibits us in some way and we unconsciously conduct our self accordingly to that hurt (real or not). This causes others to treat us based on their perception, accordingly, by our own actions / reactions. Feeling like we have no control of our external circumstances keeps that hidden insecurity alive. The Hatfield and McCoys (McCoys *were part of my heritage*) fought for years over slights and I believe became a "principle" of past disagreements rather than flowing with the times. Think of generations that keep this "principle of things" going over past hurts and slights and then add more layers as time passes!

CHAPTER 9

Flowing With Life Experience

You need to detach completely from the situation before you can heal...JS

I have always believed (*after I was mentored on self-esteem*) that illness begins from those intense emotions bottled up inside of us. After repeated body blasts from intense emotions that surface from buttons being pushed, certain blockages begin to colonize themselves in the body. In Chapter 25 I discuss how beliefs contribute to the development of colonizing impasses due to manifestation of our thoughts / decisions which turn into illness. I am speaking of embedded beliefs or habits of thinking. Often these are beliefs about what you feel is right or wrong with you. Going back to how and who raised you will of course have a big impact on how you feel about yourself.

These judgments from others combined with our own literally create a blockage in our system. The blockages begin when energy is not allowed to flow freely; if you are not taking care of yourself to start with you are already allowing weak areas to develop. This emotional process takes quite some time to become an illness but there is plenty of opportunity to turn things back into balance emotionally before a disease displays itself.

Your emotional intensity tells you when your energy is not flowing. If you continue to ignore the reasons for the intensity and consistency of outbursts, the blockage gets more prevalent. For instance you may feel upset every time you have to do a particular job. You are forcing yourself to do something that doesn't complement who you are and who you want to be. So, if you consistently ignore your hidden anger in doing things you truly don't feel good about, then the emotion embeds itself. It removes itself from your daily thoughts and expresses itself in your physical body. This repressed emotion is an energy that actually wants to be heard by you one way or the other. It will express itself through the body and finally manifest as a physical complaint. If you give it attention rather than ignore it...it releases. Again, this is not to say it is gone forever unless you are able to learn to control the intensity of outbursts as well as letting it go after all is said and done.

A physical complaint points to an emotion that you may not be aware is hovering inside you waiting to attach. I have discussed hidden angers in "The Many Faces of Self Esteem". The physical symptom makes the emotion visible to you. Physical symptoms or pain are the expression of the soul. The soul longs for communication among all of its parts. When people are in accidents or constantly damaging parts of their body by tripping, bumping into things, cutting the self, bruising self or breaking limbs, it is the soul talking to you. You are out of balance somewhere in your life.

An acquaintance, who was a maker and doer, 74 years of age and working very hard because he was in the habit to do so. He wanted to quit his job, but just couldn't bring himself to do it. He liked the extra money! He complained more and more about work because he really didn't want to be there anymore. He didn't realize he was telling his soul he had enough. So what happened, he fell, breaking a leg and thereby forcing him to be off work for several months. In the interim of his hiatus, he decided he would not go back to work. As they say, God works in mysterious ways. If he can't stop himself, God did or in essence his soul assisted in the trip. It wasn't enough damage to incapacitate him, but enough to slow him down for a bit to allow for the new decision. The soul feels quite happy with itself when there is a free flow of energy and you manifest the desires you ask for so be careful what you wish for☺. The soul becomes depressed when the energies are strangled by our constant lack of duty to ourselves or control of re-actions. Accidents occur because our soul wills it the exact way we ask for it! Our thoughts pushed the soul to manifest a solution.

Illness is a gauge: it identifies that you need heal-ing. If you identify indicators early on by learning to let go and understanding you cannot control others, you are actually cooperating with your body by preventing that emotion from embedding into your system. If you continue to never change your ways of reacting to yourself and others, aka your attitudes, the appropriated area will weaken till it isn't easily repaired *if it can at all be repaired.*

If you think of someone who has already passed on, "*before their time*", and you knew this person well enough to see the possible hidden areas of suppression or repression, you may be able to see what I am talking about. Another acquaintance, as an example, has cancer in the intestines where anger and resentment reside. I can vouch that this person had much anger and resentment from parental issues and also passed this anger to the children. He never released the anger or tried to resolve any issues. He is in stage 4 intestinal cancer.

There are people who have died instantly that everyone considered healthy. They exercised regularly and by all appearances were solid. That is the part we see. That person may have had more hidden stresses that were not visible to the normal person. People learn to wear the masks of an addiction to health as well as the opposite aspects of not taking care of ourselves. What underlying issues may this person have been dealing with…it could be perfectionist standards, labile economic issues, maintaining a certain image…if the truth were known, I feel there would be factors that caused the hidden blockages.

As I mentioned early on, the positive mental and physical picture we try to maintain can be damaged over time through excessive criticism, no support or encouragement, perceived failures or emotional abuse. The result is hidden low self-esteem masked as success. The pattern always reveals itself but this is why it is important to put yourself first or as equally important. The signs are there. Are you willing to see them? Can you detach from the old beliefs and behaviors and heal?

I will be discussing health vs. emotions in a later chapter (25). Learning to detach from these emotions, whether they are yours or inherited from the past, is absolutely necessary to keep your body in the best of shape inside and out. Trying to flow with life with no consideration of your own needs and allowing intrusion of other's opinions on 'how you need to be paying attention to their life first' can be a death sentence.

CHAPTER 10

Can You Detach?

If you love something, let it go...
if it comes back it is yours...
...if it does not, it never was
and is not meant to be.

As said in the last chapter, you need to detach completely from the situation before you can heal. I can admit I am strictly flowing right now with a general idea of where I am going with anything I am doing. I do have a structured goal but who knows where the crossroad may come that changes my direction. At times, I wonder if I should be doing more and other times I am just looking for blocks to let go of and get this free flowing thing working faster.

I am basically an impatient person and I have always known that I need to live in the present. Things cannot go faster because other pieces of the puzzle need to be in place first. So, I just keep doing what I am doing toward the goal I think I am aiming. I say "think" I am going because so far to date, I still can't know for sure what my final gift to the world and myself will be. The course gets delayed sometimes but eventually I am prompted back on track by listening to my heart.

Maybe I am already free flowing with impatience as my obstacle. My results may depend on decisions I make at the time. I may have taken the easy way at one point and had to redo a task, delayed myself due to exhaustion or I jumped in with both feet to an unknown situation that was a major risk but necessary learning lesson. Right or wrong, I don't have time to ponder the "what if's", so I just keep moving forward. If an obstacle tries to stick, I shake it off or flow through it.

I have been labeled as a "shark on blood" when I aim for anything I desire. When I was "rushing" sorority in college I went through the process, chose the one I wanted (Chi Omega) and made up my mind if I didn't get the one I wanted, I would do without. By "suiciding" as they use to call it (*which they never recommended*) I put myself in position of not getting into any sorority milieu. I felt so

strongly about the one I wanted, I was ready to detach mentally from the whole system if I did not
get what I wanted. I did end up as a Chi Omega,
but I had calmly resigned myself to another direction if I did not get in the system at all.

This is an example of detaching from the result
and allowing the desire to take its own course being satisfied either way. I would have accepted that
sorority life was just not the direction I needed to
grow if I had not been accepted. I did not opt out
for fear of not being accepted and I did not settle
for less than what I wanted in this case.

I have settled for less in other situations. My area
of relationships was one of these. My parents set
a decent example of parenting and relationships,
however "old school" it was, but I have to admit
they never really taught me anything much about
relationships. So, I have not been able to say…this
is what I want and if I don't get it…I will do without. Well, maybe I am now … I say I would rather
be alone than miserable and treated as a doormat.
So maybe I am getting there☺ I presently am detaching from finding a companion. I am detaching
from the end result by not looking. I am working
on what I need for me and releasing any blocks

to prove beyond doubt this detaching thing works. The key to detaching though, I think, is becoming a whole person first and therefore attract a whole person to me. I am burned out on saving and rescuing people and seeing the "potential" in them. Anyone with me on that?

Another obstacle for me is being an Empath. I can actually see beneath all the clutter in people and see the good part still left in them. That is why I am a very patient person to the point of accepting their issues longer than I need. The advantage to being an Empath which saves me is seeing the bullshit a mile away. The problem has been discounting my own Self to bring that good part out in them. OK...lesson learned I hope. That is not a relationship! That is a one on one therapeutic chore that I choose not to repeat in my personal life anymore. This is a very difficult task for me. It is always my test though.

People who don't want to be helped or do not know they need help have made it habitual to suck the life flow out of others and delay progress for both people involved. To some, this means extinguishing dreams you may have been nurturing were you not able to detach. Sometimes we get enmeshed for so long, we are reluctant to detach because they provided some good parts to our lives. Some people will not allow you to let go unless you figuratively change the locks. It may hurt to let go and the hardest thing to follow through with, but if you don't, you will remain stuck.

Detaching is never uncomplicated. Detaching is actually accepting change willingly. Even positive change can be challenging and frustrating. The hardest part about detaching is having to make a few steps backward and no one likes to go backwards. We concur those backward steps will cause you to finally assess if you truly needed all of the "things/people" to fill the voids you were trying to fill. It allows you to refocus your attentions back onto yourself even for a mere moment. If you learned anything, it will be a healthy step forward. If you learned nothing, you jump back into the frying pan with a different face.

You have to ground yourself before the change can progress and your level of self-esteem will identify how secure you are that things will work out for the best. I had plenty of outside input in making my changes as people have no problem inserting themselves into your plan of action directly or indirectly…but as you know this can throw you way off your path.

Sometimes we get caught up in trying to fit a square peg into a round hole and it just isn't going to fit. The person or situation is not ready for you or vice versa…you are not ready for them. Maybe both need time to grow into what is needed or it goes in a completely different direction. Perhaps it isn't supposed to fit. When a relationship or a situation has met a standstill or you keep hitting the same wall, letting the butterfly go is true love to yourself and them. Moving on until your own answer reappears is the difficult part, but it will force us to reunite with ourselves.

When you are hungry for that change, (sick and tired of being sick and tired)…the fear of the unknown begins to disappear, detachment starts and change is forthcoming. This is called surrendering as well. Things become clearer and you become obsessed in finding a way to resolve the situation. You become more assertive. You may need to back away from others for a bit to make it all work for yourself because some will sabotage or get in your way. Maybe that "support" has plenty of time off and demands your company which distracts your goals. You hate saying No, but take care of your needs first and then you can enjoy taking a day to be with them.

I had a friend that was quite demanding of my time for years. I always obliged and listened to her ranting quietly. I knew it was difficult for this person to give me space to write this book so I asked politely in advance for some space so I could complete this book among other responsibilities and also being the holidays. My time was budgeted to the second and I was still overwhelmed. The peace lasted for about a week and I started getting derogatory phone calls every 20 minutes literally. *First my cell and then my land line, back and forth.* It got so abusive and intrusive, she started calling me names. That was it for me. My line was crossed. No one calls me names for not giving them attention or for any other reason. If they cannot be patient when you ask maybe they are not good for you. If I thought this person would have insight for a mutually supportive friendship, I would try to re-establish contact. Historically, I knew this was never going to change because she feels I have the problem and not her…well adios and good luck.

First and foremost, maintain integrity for how you end things which means: You have offered all with good intentions, you have made attempts to solve the problems and you have no regrets for how you have handled things to date. You do not want to lower yourself to their level of communication and you do not need to leave a dead body with your harsh words or actions. Keep your karma slate clean, detach and look forward to your new future unencumbered!

CHAPTER 11

Resolving A Situation

The more you struggle to solve a situation,
the more you block a resolution.

Surrendering to the direction of our life by allowing life to come to us rather than chase and control the direction is ultimately our goal. This is easier said than done as we have been taught the opposite. As I have said earlier, I am also practicing the new process of allowing and it is not easy. It is very frustrating of course. The one thing I feel I have accomplished well is knowing when to let go. I used to hang on and on thinking things would change or someone would finally get it...I may let it go for a bit, but if it starts to be a pattern where I am doing all the work or making all of the effort...time to re-evaluate quickly.

In control form, your mental picture gets very narrow and focused, calculating, breath is short, adrenaline pumping and heart rate increases. I just this moment realize this is like a fight / flight mode. The mind swings from topic to topic and past to future quickly and there is little concentration, poor memory and almost no present-moment awareness.

In a surrendering mode, one is calm, seeing clearly and peacefully, breathing deeply, focusing on living in the now. Our vision can now extend all around allowing a view of the bigger picture. Attempting to control things actually feels less in control. So we worry. An example would be when one is nagging, micro-managing, or obsessing over details...we are in our own way. Surrendering literally means stop fighting with your Self. Stop fighting the universe and the natural flow of things. Stop chasing that same beach ball across the pool which always eludes our grasp causing frustration. We are resisting our own hunches which are our true reality... and allowing the misrepresented truth of others to label us as wrong.

It is not about inaction. It is about taking the action from the place of surrender energy. This is similar to my experience of "suiciding" with the sorority. I surrendered before I was chosen. I accepted I would be happy with either result. If letting go of the control (*by not being disappointed or angry if I didn't get in*) actually produces better results, how do we do that? Sometimes it is as easy as just noticing you are in control mode and choosing to let go, consciously and deliberately shifting into surrender energy.

My brothers and I used to joke about the middle brother after he made a decision that yielded less than positive results ... he would say... "oh well". We laughed for years about this. When he was learning to fly a plane and I was in the passenger seat, he made that same comment once when landing or attempting to land. I said "whoa here a minute...I don't know if hearing the words "oh well" is a good thing right now." He was totally unaffected by me, calm and just re-entered into another descending pattern which worked fine. Now I can see where this surrendering issue came into play for him in his life. To this day, he lives life in the surrendering mode with a shrug of the shoulders and a good ole "Oh well" at the end. I am sure he had his moments of exhaustion in dodging obstacles, but he came out to where he is supposed to be. He never gave up...just kept flowing.

What are you afraid of if you let go and surrender? What does it feel like? It usually feels like fear to most people. I and my brothers were basically taught to have no fear by our father even though my mother inserted the fear quality on the backside. Probably why my mother and I butted heads because I was more like my father and she was forcing me with her worry to not experience life head on.

What is the validity of that fear? If parents shelter us to where we don't experience the good and bad growing up, we tend to lean into the fear of the unknown. If something does not go our way is our whole day / life ruined? Did our parents ruin our life? Is feeling ruined a perception or a reality? We throw out words like "ruined" that really do not depict reality as we always have choice in how to react to the perceptions.

When we try to control people outside of our responsibility, it is not going to go well either. It will become part of your problem if you persist with influencing the results. Maybe you can add guidance *if asked*, but in the end it is still their final decision and responsibility to act. In half a shake you may be *enmeshed*. All of their problems now become yours and they have lost the ability to figure life out for themselves. Now they come to you for advice about everything and the blame falls on you if all is not as they hoped. You feel responsible and somewhat guilty and continue to rescue by giving things or offer more solicited misdirected advice. You may find you are in a daily spiral with no time for their excessive need for help but you created the monster! The flow has stopped for both. What is resolved?

Remember, we can only control ourselves...not others. The resolution comes from within you, not externally. This relates in both directions as the advice giver or receiver. We all know what it feels like to fall out of love or get bored with a job or relationship. Is the lack of change by staying in the situation going to ruin your life? If you allow it, yes, it will to the degree that your attitude dictates how much you are ruined or become the victim of your own inaction. No one is going to make the changes for you in the end. There will be those caretakers out there who will attempt to soften your blow by enabling your lack of growth and inaction, but it won't go on forever. Someone eventually wakes up and that guillotine hurts!

Poor resolutions are caused by burnout. Impossible deadlines, demanding bosses, abusive colleagues, unpaid overtime: all factors that can lead to a burnout. But when it comes to mental health in the workplace, the influence of home life must also be considered to get the full picture. When we try so hard to rectify it actually can get worse. We struggle and stress ourselves out trying to solve so many life situations and our mind spins with words of others on what we think we should be doing. We panic and then worry. We have talked before about thoughts and focusing on any negative thought of not having...not having is what manifests. How great would it be to stop struggling and every desire comes to you? Surrender. You can only do what you can do.

Disappointment is one of life's most uncomfortable feelings. It encompasses emotions like anger, hurt, and sadness at minimum. Separately, each emotion may be easier to handle but together we don't know which one to deal with first. It's important to learn to trust that the universe can save us from ourselves. Even though your situation might look bleak at the moment, there's something better coming. Let it go and let it happen!

We place too much emphasis on the outcome of what we envision, as opposed to enjoying the journey with detours included. We visualize that everything must be "as planned and / or should be" otherwise we are a failure: *We will have a relationship by this age, a certain job at this point, this much money in the bank by this year, this many children, this car, this house, and on and on.* We end up feeling defeated when things don't follow accordingly. Let go of your attachment to the conclusion.

When working toward any goal, we see a logical sketch of steps in our mind which usually results in a limited approach that can disappoint our motivation. What are all the options and am I open to other opportunities that appear but unplanned? It is proven our emotions, gut feelings, and unconscious minds lead to better decisions. Step away for a time if you hit a wall, shift your perception, stay open and let it simmer. The guidance will come exactly when it's meant to come. No need to search for it!

CHAPTER 12

Your Beliefs, Thoughts And Words

Believe your needs are taken care
of now and forever...JS

P eace of mind is our goal. We really do not need to earn it as it already exists. What does this mean? Why do we keep chasing that elusive beach ball in the pool? Somewhere along the line we have been taught we don't have a truth so we chase after the misguided truth of others; the truth will always elude us because it is not ours. Whether that was the intent is not important. I discussed in my first book, *The Many Faces of Self Esteem* that we acquire our esteem (our truth) from someone else in the beginning and at some point we become confused, frustrated and even angry because this truth isn't working for us and we sit and wonder what is wrong with us? We keep chasing the "hard to get hold of" beach ball that actually belongs to somebody else. The faster we chase it, the farther away it gets.

Many feel there is something wrong with them at some point in their life. I certainly remember asking the same thing of myself. You are working hard and trying to achieve in order to receive acknowledgement and consideration, maybe even a promotion, and you get over looked or stepped on as someone else cruises by you into the position or relationship you thought you had in the bag. If we observe an animal that simply exists and takes life for granted; there is no attitude of "deserving". They take the good with the bad and still are glad to see you. How do we reflect this back onto humans? It is not as simple for us to wag our tail at someone that disregarded your value.

We always have permission to receive and enjoy what we receive, but this happens only when we love ourselves and accept that corrupt things are going to happen. It doesn't affect your soul. It is part of making your pearl. The good and bad are part of the whole. We have been conditioned to believe a certain way which many times sabotage our own progress by just the power of the words we use.

This isn't a new concept but a very important one. I have a friend who doesn't have a positive thing to say about anyone...he wishes he could find someone that knows how to cut hair or a doctor who knew what he was doing or a family member that isn't good enough to be part of the inner circle. The negative is prevalent for everything. Wonder why? Other statements we hear / say consistently *even as subtle as the thought may be:*

- I never have any money
- I can't get ahead
- I look at food and get fat
- Nothing goes my way
- I am never getting any better
- I always attract the wrong people
- Why do they get everything and I get nothing
- I have the worst luck
- Why does this keep happening to me?

These are statements why people do not get very far in life because they are constantly telling themselves they are not capable of doing / having it. Everything you say or think you are branding into your subconscious. I actually have been observing a Narcissist lately and wondering how he seems to get everything handed to him whether in a

relationship or in business. It is almost unbeliev-
able the opportunities that flow to him.

Per chance, he believes he deserves it as he never
seems to accept less. Of course, too much of anything becomes a weakness and this includes being
self-affirming. The dead bodies left behind isn't
confirming and they end up being alone in the
end because no one can stand to be around them.
Yet, if we take a lesson from observing them... what
is working? They get opportunity to make money,
have power and fabulous beginning relationships,
but they can't always maintain the façade forever
as people begin to put two and two together. That
selfish ego vampire always surfaces. They may be
in great shape physically by working out every day
but they constantly struggle emotionally by feeding
off the energy and necessary adoration of others.
Have to beat the Jones! These are one faction of
people having the heart attacks or strokes. Their
belief of life existence eludes peace of mind because they are too busy filling voids for the sake of
image.

The belief about being "the one and only and
perfect in every way" in a sense... works. The opportunities definitely come. He definitely doesn't

compare himself to others as a person (why should he as he is perfect) but only in what he wins. I honestly have never heard him say one of the negative statements in the above list. The problem is he is never content and like I said has burnt many bridges to get where he is now. He doesn't even wonder why he has to keep moving on in relationships and jobs. He just keeps moving. He has convinced himself he is right and everyone else has the problem. It becomes his belief and a way of life, right or wrong.

Your beliefs mold your life more than anything. Most do not take the time to know what works for our Self and we haul around all of the dysfunction we have mostly inherited, not always learned. When your beliefs are iffy, unclear or non-existent...self-doubt, lack of self-trust, poor self-image, low self-esteem begins to surface. This is where most people make mistakes with their affirmations. The affirmations you are drawn to use are usually the exact opposite of your belief. Change your belief and the affirmations start to work where you may not even need the affirmation any more.

Repeating affirmations with no emotional feeling for the goal will not manifest the success you desire.

Your thoughts / word choices are a spinoff of your present belief system. If these beliefs contradict the affirmations you are telling yourself, you are using a formula for failure. So you need to evaluate your beliefs if you want to make serious changes in your thoughts and your ability to manifest success. Go out and experience what you want to manifest and actually feel that desire! Write down when and how often you block or minimize that desire with your old words and thoughts by checking one of the above negative comments you find yourself saying over and over. Maintain integrity of belief with yourself when creating the new belief! It is simple but not easy changing a lifetime of negative thought and word conditioning.

Every time you make a decision, check it against your present beliefs and make sure the two are on the same wavelength. This sets the pace for your thoughts and words to follow. If your belief about having money is negative because you feel people with money are condescending, then the affirmation of money coming to you will be blocked by this thought. Your belief will overpower your affirmation. Do this exercise backwards. Write an affirmation and then next to it write your present value or belief on that subject as you were taught or have to come to feel. See how they differ or what might be blocking you from receiving!

To change and improve your self-esteem, you need to believe and create confidence in decisions through new experiences; not just repeat one expression over and over about how perfect you really are as an affirmation suggests we do. Affirming thoughts are helpful because they challenge you and help re-program your views on things. However allowing your doubts to interfere or someone sets you back by making a perceived belittling comment will cause you to remain where you started. Allow the affirmation you desire to identify your new positive belief and if that belief needs to change to fit the affirmation, your results will change accordingly after the change in belief.

When considering steps for a positive change in life, most people feel that sacrifice, discipline, and effort plays a big role. Yes, you may need this structure to make it happen, but if you do not feel a passion and belief in what you are doing, you could slide off the path by any diversion. You hold the magic wand by going at a pace you can handle. Give yourself permission to have fun if you want, allow for short diversions but do not let others insert themselves into your plans to keep you off balance. The stresses now are too great to not find your balance. You can even burn your passion out. Their words can become your words if not monitored against your own vibration pattern.

It doesn't require giving up anything to start (maybe someone/s); it encourages you to say something positive to yourself to be able to stay on your track. You don't need everything to be perfect before you start or anyone else's approval. Just start. The less you tell people what you are doing, the less you hear the naysaying opinions☺. The more you tell people what you are doing means you are looking for validation from them and we don't need their validation anymore, remember? We are seeking our own validation from our own thoughts, words and beliefs. This will have to be a conscious mind control game with your Self as it is so easy to fall into their webs of sabotage. In time, it gets easier when your passion is strong. This is the peace of mind we speak.

CHAPTER 13

You Are A Reflection of Your Thoughts

Your body hears everything your mind says.
NAOMI JUDD

We have talked about affirmations and our thoughts in previous chapter. Everyone has planned exactly where they are to date. I know some are disagreeing with me right now, but fortunately it is true. Our own thoughts whether learned from someone else or by our decisions create our reality. Where the fork in the road occurs... we have let other's thoughts infiltrate our minds without testing the truth for ourselves and it becomes our thought. Many times, as I have mentioned, these thoughts are passed down through generations and we just keep going with that flow thinking it is what it is.

For every feeling we have a thought that parallels. It can be either positive or negative. Our esteem is then measured on how that thought made us feel. So having positive thoughts will generate better feelings. Simple, right? Therefore, to truly understand self-esteem is to be able to revise our thoughts to create what we want which hopefully is a positive result, not damaging. We try to change our thoughts with our affirmations, but other's get involved in our thought processes and it seems we keep swimming upstream.

These vague reflections of surreal goals lead to low self-esteem and can contribute to anxiety, stress, loneliness, depression, problems with relationships, seriously impair educational and job functioning and also generate an increased susceptibility to drug and alcohol abuse and dependency. Quite a bit of influence for self – esteem, wouldn't you say? A person with positive self-esteem tends to be more focused in creating a happy and healthy life and living honestly. We have to work at both aspects to make them real. Yes both.

Many of you had families who were non-nurturing and / or unappreciative of whom you were / are... This subliminally left deep emotional scars on you.

They are not you! These scars remain as a reflection even as the adult. This is part of developing your pearl. The reflection you see is through their mirror. Let go of those descending visions and buy a new mirror you like to look into now.

So what happens when we listen to others? We tend to absorb the energy coming from them because we are energy: The friend who is always negative or opinionated with nothing positive to say; the nagger who nit-picks everything…the media playing on tragedy because it sells. We react with horror, sadness or anger at what we hear and this energy pounds on us daily. We become fearful over time and yet nothing has really happened directly in our personal world. We comment "what is the rest of the world coming to"? We assume this didn't occur *"back in the day"* …but is that because we just didn't hear about? We justify our negative views from reflections of the rest of the world? So now we have people selling us things to make us feel safer, but has it changed the world? Is our esteem any better? Now we are afraid to come out of our houses. The reflections are scaring us now.

In tandem to this theory, an individual may think, for example, he is "worthless" or "a loser" and as a result will tend to perpetuate low self-esteem by making and experiencing poor decision results. *Ye ole "self-sabotage"* routine appears over and over. Others send you their "perceptional" energy assumptions reflecting what they see happening to you over and over. What stops you from continuing on through their energy blocks to feel success? Probably someone you trusted has set or had set self-limiting beliefs in the past for you and transferred all their inherited "reflections of lack" to you in one way or another.

You receive fears from others everyday whether you want to or not and it builds up to overload. It can make you irritable and now YOU are emanating negative vibes. Over time, it becomes part of you because it never lets up; now a belief is forming, which affects your thoughts and then follows your self-perceived low esteem due to the negative energy flow through you. Now life appears as it has in the past and the future will become probably more of the same. Voila! Hopelessness!

Any negative thought a person has about himself with already poor self-esteem accepts negative opinions about who he thinks he is. Unless this core thought or belief a person has about himself is changed or transformed, he will continue to experience a negative self-esteem level and as a result will generate life experiences that match and validate what they reflect about themselves. Continuing this lifestyle pattern will manifest the same as it has in the past and one's future will merely be the probable almost certain future of the same. Again, hopelessness!

We discussed the process of working affirmations. These can be a very powerful tool for transforming what a person thinks and feels and as a result improve the individual's self-esteem. Consistent use of positive affirmations that align with new beliefs will assist in transforming old life patterns and alter the volume of your inner voice. This begins a transformation from low self-esteem tradition to finding that hidden positive esteem we thought never existed. But remember, focus on identifying what your belief is before you start the affirmations. If they are not in alignment, you are just saying words that reflect your belief.

From experience, utilizing positive affirmations will be more effective when using therapeutic relaxation music. *Relaxation* music enhances the effect of positive feelings that create a very relaxed environment for the individual to become even more open to the new beliefs. I listen to music as I write. (*Set aside alone time consistently for this.*) Let the music and your new beliefs about yourself absorb into your system at the same time. It has taken many years to reinforce the negative; so again, it is not an overnight process. You have believed all is true because your experiences have validated where your thinking stands to date. You have to be the one to embrace the act of changing. You cannot be waiting for that someone else to do it for you. If you allow someone else to control you, you may have opened yourself up to the predatory narcissist. No Bueno. Hopefully now after 75 pages of reading you can see magic lies within your reflections you have of yourself.

CHAPTER 14

What Just Happened to Me?

> *"What are you talking about?"*
> *Narcissus demanded.*
> *"I am amazing. Everyone knows this."*
> *"Amazing at pure suck," Leo*
> *said. "If I was as suck as you,*
> *I'd drown myself.*
> *Oh wait, you already did that."*
> — RICK RIORDAN, THE
> MARK OF ATHENA

I find this topic to be of utmost importance to those of us who have a trusting heart and a kindness to give and express love by giving more than receiving. This was a hard and expensive lesson for me I hate to admit. I am presently, as I write this book, recently detached from the tentacles of one who is a vampire in so many ways.

There are those people who exist that are preda-
tors on our kind. Yes, they really do exist! This
could be a continued problem for me as I said I am
empathic as well, so I see beyond the screwed up
parts of people to the core of where love still exists
in them and I forget that I still have to deal with
the screwed up parts.

I am also educating myself in regard to this type situation and I have to say if I did not work in the field
of psychology, I am not sure I would have figured
these people out... *ever.* They are good at what they
do. My heart is feeling very sad for these people,
this person, the Narcissist. I used to think a narcissist was just a person with a big ego that basically was
all about them self. Well, that part is still true, but
as I dig deeper into this disorder, I am saying WOW!

I am not a clinician with regard to this topic, only
one who has experienced living with one. I do
know self-esteem and I find the Narcissist is truly
void of esteem. They have no self. Surprised?
Before I get into what I think I know, I also understand the only cure is therapy. Recovery entails
improving boundaries and self-acceptance which is
no easy task. There is no medication per se to cure
an ass. The problem is they don't think they have a

problem so chances are we will encounter them all over the place. So what do we do? They are slowly killing us by emotional abuse, financial abuse, and any other abuse that sucks the life from us.

It's easy to never detect or even be aware you are walking into a trap of a narcissist and then you fall in love with one. Their charm, apparent success, and charisma is a magic charm, along with their over-board compliments that address the very thing you need to hear. They are witty with conversation and what seems a sincere interest and respect that seems too good to be true. Once captivated by them and they are sure you are hooked, you see another side appear in time: demands, criticisms, disrespect and selfishness. First, they start with the condescending "jokes" about being blonde or being hit on the head when you were a child. Then the conversation starts to revolve around them, their wants and needs and they start bossing you around...could be in a fun way or not...same result in the end. Now you do not have a smart thing to say or now you do not have a thought in your head according to them, so be quiet, the Narcissist is talking!

In the beginning, you were delighted to be in the narcissist's aura. They sound protective and make you feel all your worries will melt away. They do enough and make promises that excite you because you have been missing all of that. Little do you know they have researched you by asking all the questions first and because we are not suspecting anything, we give them all the answers. It takes time to realize what is happening, *that pattern,* but in time, you become tense and drained from unpredictable tantrums, attacks, and unjustified offenses at invented slights. You start to wonder when the promises are coming true. Their contentment always seems to be out of reach for you because of some new slight someone has done to them.

You feel sorry again and somehow you doubt yourself, worry what they think, and become as pre-occupied with them trying to figure out their next mood. You try to escape but they keep you off balance with a few good comments that keep you attached. You start to walk on eggshells because you never know what is going to set them off and you get to the point of saying nothing which is their goal because they are sucking your life from you! Now they have control.

A narcissist sees the world and everything that happens through self-centered eyes. This can be a guy or girl. They have little regard for feelings of spouses, children or friends almost to point of no remorse you realize. They cannot handle criticism (clue) and cannot persevere through hard times without a safety net to cushion their fall. Therefore, they are always looking for a backup safety net if the one they have wises up. The safety net becomes an unsuspecting new relationship with a stable and financially secure person or at least they are stable until they meet the narcissist. They give their tale of woe at how their last companion was an alcoholic or a person of drama and they couldn't take it anymore. You suck it all in and say, "I'll save you because I am not like that". "You can rest your head knowing life will be different"…oh boy, how wrong you are. It will be the same because the narcissist plans on doing it all over again. Some of you may be saying…oh lord, I think I might know someone or I am living with this too.

It could be just a big ego. Sometimes it is difficult to distinguish a high-functioning narcissist from someone with "just a big ego". Every narcissist has a big ego but not every big ego is a narcissist. We all start out as narcissistic infants and we retain a degree of it as we develop and a little of it is good to hold onto. There is a part of them that manifests things so easily and I want to capture that skill! I think how do they do this? Briefly, I will say because they have no fear they can't get what they want. They feel they are the best: they say all the right things, the image looks the part, but they just can't hold onto anything for long because people cannot tolerate this god that tramples on everyone to get where they are going and the pattern eventually shows itself. I always say, their karma, not mine. I have maintained my integrity and I can live with the mistakes I made whether I knew I was making them or not.

After being continually chastised along with the intermittent charm to keep you off balance, you start to lose self-confidence. You may have had self-esteem when you met, but your significant other alludes to you always coming up short, and doesn't fail to point it out. They never listen to your advice, and tell you that you either do not understand what they are saying or the thought was stupid; but they hear the same idea from someone else makes it a great idea now! NOTHING you or others do is right or appreciated. They goad you into talking about your hurts, then turn all around on you to where it is your fault. It is a sick place to be for them and you.

It's difficult to be empathetic with narcissists, but they didn't choose to be that way. Their development was stifled as a toddler due to non-nurturing parents, usually by the mother who didn't / couldn't provide sufficient encouragement due to being a single mother with several jobs or maybe one of the parents was also a narcissist that didn't show the nurturing because again, life is about them. The child is left with an unrealistic view of themselves on how they are to become. There has been no development of their Self, so they learn to live off the lives of others. They learn no boundaries and see others as an extension of themselves.

An example would be if you own a house, they moved in and all of sudden it becomes their house even though their name is not on the mortgage or lease. Your money becomes their money even though you are not married or even in a relationship. You're on call to meet their needs in whatever way they need – it could be a comment like "You can buy me golf clubs for my birthday...wouldn't that be fun for you?" or ask you to purchase something and they will pay you back later, but the payback never happens.

You might get caught-up in trying to please them because you feel sorry or you want to provide what they didn't have, but it is like trying to fill a bottomless pit. Their needs, whether for admiration, service, love, or purchases, are infinite. I always used to say high maintenance. They can fall into feelings of hopelessness or rage if they encounter failure, rejection or you say NO, and yet they feel unconquerable when they meet with victory. They don't like to hear "No" and setting boundaries threatens them! They'll manipulate to get their way and devalue you because you didn't read their mind. Nevertheless, you stay in the relationship, because periodically the charm, excitement, and loving gestures that first enchanted you return temporarily.

Is it possible for Narcissists to love? In the community, narcissists switch on the magnetism that first drew you in. People gravitate towards them and are enlivened by their buoyant passionate energy. You're feeling proud, but at home, they're totally different as we have already discussed. They may also privately defame a person they were just praising at a party. Now you feel they trust you enough to confide their feelings to you!

There is misconception of them feeling "perfect". Actually they dislike themselves immensely. Their inflated self-flattery, perfectionism, and superiority are merely covers for the self-loathing they won't admit –even to themselves. Instead, it's projected outwards in their disregard for and criticism of others. This is why they don't want to look at themselves. They're too afraid, because they believe that the truth would be devastating. Actually, they don't have much of a Self at all. Emotionally, they're dead inside. This is sad and also dangerous.

Usually they have an emotionally empty parent, who faithfully attached to them when they were a child to survive because the other parent was absent. That existing parent made the child into what the parent needed emotionally. That deprivation of real nurturing and lack of boundaries between child and existing parent make future narcissists dependent on others to feed their insatiable need for validation. They don't know themselves, but only can love themselves as a reflection in the eyes of others and the emotions they interpret back to themselves. The way they are truly feeling is how they try to make you feel and then their existing truth is validated when the negative responses reflect back to them. These people lack a core Self, and define themselves based on others. This is true for all narcissists to a varying degree, whose Self is so weak and insecure, they need CONSTANT validation.

A big ego has self-confidence and realistic expectations and is generally healthy. It is not exaggerated and phony. A big ego is not a bad thing. They have realistic and consistent successes, definite self-esteem, and the ability to get through difficult times by flowing and staying focused on their goals without destroying everyone around them. They don't become hopeless when they meet with failure or have feelings of superiority when they are triumphant. They are able to see the obstacles, find a solution on their own in the face of adversity. Like the sure footed goat or burrow on a steep mountainside carrying a load of other baggage. They will make it.

I apologize if this was lengthy, but these types are difficult to pinpoint and if you think you had self-esteem, you probably did before you met them. Thank God I had decent self-esteem and have been studying self-esteem for a long time. I still got caught off guard, but alas it was a necessary learning curve for me. I could sense his trying to chip away at me little by little, but I couldn't pinpoint the source other than self-esteem issue. I kept thinking I could work with him and make it right....lol. Alas, it was a battle with "no self-esteem" which I cannot win without him making his own effort. So I made it clear to him he would not win by trying to break me.

So my advice, if you are lucky enough to not be with one, don't be crazy enough to put everything you own, your high salary and financial status on FB and Match.com to impress. You are a sure fired target. If you are already with one...you had best work on your own esteem *in private,* and get out! Plug up the financial holes, stop giving more than you are getting and stand up for yourself. Eventually, they will look for the next source and leave you alone. Good riddance until they face themselves, if that ever happens☹

I always have hope they will realize and take the steps to correct the problems, but it will take a crash for them to give up and try. If they are fed continuously by some unknowing person with a good heart, they will continue to feed. Don't let it be off you. Life is too short to live the rest of it in misery! This is just abuse!

CHAPTER 15

Abusing Love?

Bullies want to abuse you.
Instead of allowing that,
you can use them as your
personal motivators.
Power up and let the bully eat
your dust! **Nick Vujicic**

Abusive people make sure their victims suffer in silence. You might love them so much you will adjust your behavior to whatever they ask of you (*what they ask changes all the time, so you will never 'do or be enough'*)... It's no wonder you are deceived because it starts out so subtly. And no, you are not stupid - it could have happened to anyone and has happened to even the strongest of personalities! When the emotions are involved, every slight is perceived initially with unconditional acceptance. We are taught to love all of them! Over an extended period of abuse, it will contaminate your definition of trust. We know without trust, relationships are on the down slope of failing anyway. Abuse coming from a family member who has your "best interests" at heart magnifies the self-imposed negative emotions of guilt and being very confused about trusting love.

We have discussed the different type abuses, but in reality, they all follow the same protocol. They present well in public, and then come home to abuse you. They will make you think you are crazy and paranoid and say things like "I don't even know you anymore"…I don't like what I see"… "you will be alone all your life if you keep that up", "Don't tell anyone or I will have to hurt them"; or they could go to another extreme and tell you no one loves you, but they do and they are just trying to help.

The abuser eventually reveals the real person inside. They are a charmer and smooth talker. They could have played the role as charming, caring, sensitive and loving - early in relationship. They start the jokes about you being a blonde or did you ride the little yellow bus when you were young as we mentioned earlier. I believe another joking comment I have heard is "Did you get hit on the head when you were young"? These comments can surface in a social gathering just as easily as at home because they still border joke / abusive. People laugh with them unaware of what follows for you.

Over time, the 'innocent' questions and comments begin. "Why do you want to go out or stay in touch with so-and-so"? Why would you want to belong in this or that activity? They may give you the silent treatment when you have gone out with friends. You'll soon be questioning yourself. Humm, sound familiar to anyone so far?

Abusers use strong prejudiced logic to condition their victims into making no comment because they make it obvious they are passionate about the comment and who needs to battle over something that is an opinion. At this point, you feel you can let it slide and you even like their strong attitude at first! The abuser next will start making trivial requests to insure they have power over you and see if you will do as they say. This would begin ma- nipulation of the mind and slow destruction of the victim's esteem by chipping away little by little and over a period of time when you don't "do it right".

Giving you advice on how to adjust or change the results become the utensils for their mind manipulation because you never feel you can do it to their 100% liking.

This can escalate over time to possibly limiting your social interaction by keeping you busy or doing what they want you to do. Ever make plans and all of a sudden they had plans for you on the same day and time, so now you have to make a choice! They become extremely agitated or angry when they don't get their way. So you do what they planned to keep peace.

They may even express jealousy or possessiveness. How romantic, right? You may get questioned where you are going, who you are going with, what your plans are and when you will be home. Wow, they really care! You start to become mentally dependent on them to run your life. Depending on the relationship they could eventually threaten you in some way like a "take-away"-threat...money, credit cards...etc if you do not comply. Just another way to control you and make you feel like you are begging. And right when you are ready to explode, they do something nice for all your hard work! Now you are all off balance!

Abusers can't seem to develop close, satisfying re-lationships or even make a bad relationship last. Wonder why? They replace intimacy with drama in order to make their life more exciting. They love watching others squirm, argue and fight and often do things to keep one in a state of constant cha-os and upheaval. I have seen where a spouse will keep the other so busy cleaning up their messes; the spouse has no time to do anything else. The abuser then minimizes their actions and refuses to acknowledge their mistakes or stirring up any-thing. In fact, they don't recall anything!

These are but a few of the traits you may or not be living with or around. This is not easy to get out of on your own unless you have all of your ducks in a row financially and supportively. I plead that you find assistance in this matter especially if you feel threatened physically. Even though this is a self-esteem issue on both sides, we are talking about serious and chronic self-esteem issues that could cause harm. You feel betrayed and kick yourself for believing in their love.

We feel very wronged when people believe someone who twists the truth about us. If an unfamiliar person believes a lie about us, we aren't too surprised, and it is understandable even though it makes us angry. But if someone we know believes that same lie, we feel betrayed. They have betrayed us by believing that lie about us. You can't believe it because your old friends know you, so no one should be able to come along and tell them *just anything* about you.

Over the years, your behavior ought to be grounded with regard to your honesty, integrity and sensible response to situations. These pot stirrers try to strip your life from you just to see if they can. They come along, hit your hot buttons, step back and say "see, I told you so...she is crazy". Now your character is being attacked. Your friends should know better, but the lie is scandalous and people gravitate toward gossip like that. The one positive thing I can say is you find out who your true friends are...this is another form of abuse. All you do is shake your head in disbelief and wonder what just happened.

If you have the gumption to confront them, it is usually followed by an arrogant, smug demeanor like the cat that ate the canary. Purposeful malicious attitude flows so easily from them. Never give them the satisfaction they won. To continue their advantage, they will put you down, blame you, ignore you, and/or ridicule you behind your back and to your face. When you plead, cry, scream, rant and rave, they will receive the response with smug indifference. Someone with shaky self-esteem will feel so powerless. You feel nothing is heard, nothing is felt, nothing is given any credibility or respect, and certainly there is no caring. And you are right, they don't care! NOTHING justifies this behavior!

The only surviving factor is maintaining your own integrity. As I say, it is their Karma, not yours. Maintain your sanity and your goals and find a way out. Accept your part in this failed relationship and move on. Give them no information to use against you, no emotional responses and hopefully they will move on to the next person. There is no way out except total termination of the relationship. If you are in a position that you have no money or anywhere to go (which is possible depending on how much control they have had on you)...please seek help. There are so many options. Then, begin to start work on yourself so you do not fall into the same situation again.

CHAPTER 16

Toxic Love

To live is to choose. But to choose well,
you must know who you are
and what you stand for,
where you want to go and why
you want to get there.
— KOFI ANNAN

Many people have accepted a false interpretation of what true love really means. For such a long time, when true love appears to knock, we initially have a tendency to ignore and allow potential nuisances (red flags) to slide by unnoticed because we have been taught to forgive and forget and nobody is perfect; otherwise they have "good points" that we tend to attach ourselves to and fall into the mindset of accepting the parts we do like as the basis for loving. As we have discussed, when we feel we are in love, we will love them for all their flaws….that true love is hard work. I disagree with this last statement, but I can't expect others to follow me on that yet.

Some may not believe or accept that love exists because they have experienced toxic love for so long living in dysfunctional type families and relationships, it becomes normal to not love or think love is supposed to be this way. We are basically trusting that we need to persevere and one day the abuser will see their negative ways. We can identify people that run from love with one foot out the door by never committing or self-sabotage by giving to the point of rescue when you need to rescue yourself.

Many have been polluted with these continued dashed expectations, needs and fears of perpetrators trying to grab on and modify the good natured by bringing them down to a low level of conduct groveling to hold on. What are you actually holding on to? The kind hearted become comfortable being uncomfortable or maybe they have lost the strength to even try and just give up and accept things as they are "meant to be". Only until they are sick and tired of being sick and tired will anything change! By this time, you may not care what happens and your once positive view of life is weighted down by the perceived reality of more of the same.

There are basically two different types of love umbrellas, of course, with spokes making up each umbrella. I am not going to cover all the spokes, but
know all the spokes hold each umbrella together.
There is puppy love, friend love, and all the loves
that are not a threat to us in such a magnanimous
way as the love of trusting someone you want to
feel safe with forever. The main love which encompasses the two umbrellas is self-love. Let us discuss
the two umbrellas since that is where we are stuck.
Once we unstick this, the self-love will be easier.

We have the two umbrellas which cover the two
main kinds of love: *true love and ego love.* Ego love
comes from what we think we want and true love
from the heart. Examples of Ego love might be
the "charm on the arm", the prestigious job/mon-
ey someone has or the car they drive. It is what
we can accumulate from someone to make us look
good in the eyes of others. We will talk about this
later.

Ego is the thinking side which conditioned us
through commercials or ads for what is acceptable
and cool. This conditioning doesn't care what
works but what sells. So, yes, it takes hard effort
to make a relationship work based on these false

pretenses of what is acceptable! The ego is always looking to send its love elsewhere as well as receive love from elsewhere. It is fear based by 'not having' or losing something.

True love is just "being". It is feeling. It is easy, warm, cozy, fun and comfortable. Any disagreements involve solutions that are win-win, non-degrading and unselfish. You have nothing to prove to anyone or be on stage when you don't want to "play the role". True love also has to be taught ... we have already learned about ego based love and how is that working for us? Even as a youngster I never understood why people said you have to work at love. It made no sense to me. I even tried to do it their way. "Forgive and forget, accept the flaws and move on, nobody is perfect"...somehow I think / know there are some big holes missing in this philosophy. The divorce rates are up; families breaking apart, suicides are higher than natural deaths. Apparently, the struggles are too great in trying to make it work and all because we are ego based with our love perceptions!

If you are afraid of being by yourself, you are already alone. We have always been encouraged to be with other people, but being alone is actually a good time to ground yourself and remember what you are about and what you enjoy doing for yourself. What do you do with that "alone time"? When we spend so much time filling our time by doing for others and go, go going...how do we take time to stay in touch with ourselves? We lose ourselves. After my divorce, I went to grocery to buy food for myself. I couldn't believe I was having a conversation with myself on what I wanted! I spent so many years thinking about what others wanted to eat. I felt like a kid in a candy store. I actually wanted healthier food, too, I noticed!

When you are lonely, you are constantly looking to fill a "nothingness" that eats away at you. You are used to having that external stimulation (ego based) to keep you moving forward or backward as the case may be...self-esteem is low either way. You crave something that no longer exists for you or maybe never existed and you want what you can never have... in your mind. Have you ever heard someone say that so-and-so thrives on chaos? Even chaos fills a void. One is never satisfied being by oneself and always looking for the external "void filling of the moment". This can enable others to jump right in to help you fill your voids by wasting your time and energy because they are in worse shape than you … or the workaholic or any …"oholic" statuses bubble to the surface to fill the empty space of time.

You are basically saying I do not want to take time to find out what is missing for me. Learning to be "alone" can be peaceful. You are focusing on your likes and dislikes. Now you can attract the right person because you no longer need to accept nonsense and fill yourself up with "stuff" that is not yours or not acceptable to you! Watch the Never Ending Stories by Disney…it is all about nothingness. Actually quite profound as all Disney movies I feel.

We have to make our own choices on which love we want. It is always our choice. Can you imagine love without conditions or expectations where everyone is in harmony and solving any obstacles that arise together? No one judges when you screw up and they are willing to take the time to listen and process with you together? You want to give rather than take. This is true love. We need not accept anything less. There will always be obstacles, but true love will allow for them and seek solutions that are win-win.

Ego love creates attitudes, expectations, blaming others, suffering, fights, friction and just plain old causing more problems where hurt and anger stem. There will always be conditions with ego love and yet people seem to accept this and maintain that resistance is easier by changing others to meet standards that don't even exist. If we had standards, we wouldn't be in this mess. Of course, it is easier to see the flaws in others and make believe that standards are there.

Some crave attention (attention seekers) because they feel without it, they are nothing. This can involve the parental guidance which can be misinterpreted and acted out as tough love or the neglect of teaching at all. Tough love needs to teach, but not at the expense of making anyone feel less than for not knowing and causing a person to spend the rest of their lives trying to get approval from someone, anyone to fill that void of self-love. If you grew up with parents who continually betrayed this trust, a part of your healing is learning to trust yourself so you can trust others again.

If you do not learn that you can trust in you for all you need to feel good, then you will constantly be striving for someone's approval which may never come. This can come as acting out, self-medicating to numb yourself, or even promiscuity to feel loved which always backfires. You are riddled with toxic thinking.

People often worry about what others will think. We ask questions. "If I am alone, is something wrong with me? If I don't date, do people think I am unhappy? Do we ever acknowledge that we need to work on the relationship with our Self? There is a defect that "self" does not get the same urgent attention. So, we settle for less than harmonious just because we want someone in our lives to fill a perceived void. Therefore you settle for the fights and bickering and disharmonious environments.

One issue is people who get caught up being a "pick-up artist" or the "schmoozer / user" as I say. A pick up artist uses subtle deception with words to hook the vulnerable–usually to have sex in the end. As I have said before, once the hook is in, they start to show their true colors but the victim is already hooked and starts to go blind. The manipulation of a sad story grips your heart or words that promise everything you are lacking. They "get you" emotionally or so it seems. I have mentioned this in an earlier chapter and once all is comfortable, wham...things change. You didn't see the one foot out the door or recognize the vague avoidant response to a serious question. They will even convince you they were upfront with you and now it is your fault.

What the schmoozers don't understand is they are totally a victim of their own hidden expectancy for finding happiness but they are actually manipulating themselves. They start running from you trying to change/save them and the fighting starts. It is part of the MO and remember… they have to do the changing. The time frame for hanging around and sucking one dry depends on the esteem of the rescuer and how long it is allowed to continue. Rest assured they will find another victim, so don't be the one to endure their nonsense. I repeat this scenario because we need to see there are so many ways to get hooked.

If you allow ego based thinking to direct your decisions, you will keep falling in and out of love with the pain of betrayals and repetitive type of abuses. There is nothing wrong with trial and error if you learn more about yourself so the future decisions are more wisely made. Needing approval of others will stop the process of finding true love.

CHAPTER 17
Needing Approval

People who want the most
approval get the least
and people who need approval
the least get the most.
— WAYNE DYER

The need for approval kills your freedom. The most important concept to understand about this is: what you need from others is what you need to heal within yourself. We rarely stop and think about this but you actually can drain others to fill the void of what is missing in you usually to the point that pushes them away. Once you identify the missing part of you that needs healing, you'll no longer need it from others, therefore allowing more freedom to grow. It's the blind spot that stops you and drains them.

We just finished talking about examples of the ego based loving and needing that approval certainly qualifies as ego based. Love you think you acquire is by what the norm expects and advertises to you. What you think you are missing becomes a goal. We all were created perfect in the eyes of God, so why do you doubt that anything is missing? Again, we have been taught that we have missing pieces by the words said to us..."you are a loser, you will never be anything, love does not exist, accept less because look what happens to the people with money...they are greedy and snobbish. Toxic thinking again!

When you are needy, you need the adoration of the other person for your own security no matter how you get it. Bad behavior to get attention falls right in there as well. Take a look at the person you need approval from and decide if they are worthy of you losing your identity and being unhappy just to please them. Dependence on others' approval calls into play more use of control and power to get it. To the degree a person needs someone is equal to the demand of needing to control his / her time / behavior. Some forms of this controlling element can be jealousy, demands, abuse, fault-finding, expectations, etc.

This now begins the destructive relationship! To give up your individuality is obviously destructive to both parties. True love between two people shows they can be self-sufficient from each other and respect any differences. They can come together out of "want", not needs. Forcing them to fulfill your needs or forcing them to accept your ways creates struggle and we know now this is not the goal.

Pay attention to your own actions. For example, you volunteer with a well-known charity. Now, when you think about helping this group, what do you think about? Do you need someone to feel proud or respectful of you when they hear about it or are you doing it just to help? If it is to gain approval ask yourself what you really need. If it's respect, then explore that aspect of yourself. Once you feel respect for yourself (*not from external sources and kudos*), you will not need respect from others. Pay attention to why you get involved in so many activities! This is not to say you don't create charities to help those in need, just pay attention to why you are doing it. I was taught if you truly help even one person, it is worth the effort...not whether it was a mass success or failure and/or will people now respect me.

The need for approval will negatively influence your performance and ultimately your integrity— you procrastinate, avoid doing important things for fear of making a mistake, feel anxiety and fear, and get stuck in worry and rumination because others will judge. Wanting people to like you causes declining new opportunities because you are missing the cues. You are so busy focusing on gratifying others or being gratified you become too anxious to function effectively which can show up as signs of avoidance, apathy, withdrawal, analysis paralysis, or giving up. It can also cause you to do things that may not be so appropriate where integrity is questioned. You lose either way.

If this rings true for you, focus upon how the need for approval is holding you back from doing the important things. Once you move past this, you will be free to achieve and create what you want in life with much less stress and effort, because you are currently exhausting yourself by avoiding the hidden aspects of your own needs. Identify how much you really need approval…You feel "you are not good enough, need more money to prove your validation, avoid hurting others' feelings by avoiding conflict, hide from the truth, people pleasers, over responsible, wait for others who are always late, depend on others for everything, and give up your own wants and needs to please others."

If you want more money it is because you deserve to have it. Your time is valuable, so what is a reasonable time to wait for someone who is always late? Why should I avoid hurting another person's feeling who just hurt mine? Why do I keep pleasing people and I get nothing in return? These are questions to really ask of yourself. You can put yourself first in these solutions by setting a boundary that you are happy with and verbalize your value to them with integrity of course.

You may be a high achiever and get great results in your life, but is it at the expense of everything and everyone including yourself. The need for approval in these cases can result in doing too much, creating anxiety, worrying, being unable to stop your mind from running at high speed, loss of sleep, trying to please everyone, not making time for yourself, working too hard, and being unable to say no because of the rush it gives your ego. You can become irritable, short, demeaning, and even narcissistic where you never can do wrong... because it is obviously their fault when something goes wrong or you have been busting your bottom to make things happen and they are not. If this is you, focus upon how the need for approval is causing you to do too much! What is your true goal?

You need to practice seeking out validation internally for your choices and most importantly, for whom you choose to be. The more you need validation externally, the more your esteem needs some work and that is ok…that is our purpose… to find that which brings us true peace for ourselves and acceptance without judgment toward others.

Some other examples of needing validation: fear of being judged causes the need to be validated, impressing others by trying too hard, reading something into what was "implied", injecting your opinion or allowing them to control you with their opinion, being overly polite for validation, afraid of saying something for fear of sounding stupid or giving too much information hoping they accept you more.

You will feel an overwhelming sense of relief when you don't need to be on stage or justify your existence / decisions. You need to be able to enjoy conversations with others without stressing yourself out trying to think of something ingenious to say. You won't interrupt people and will calmly let them finish their sentences; you won't be tuning out, or apologize and make excuses for your actions. This will all instantly disappear when you no longer need approval from others. Voilà! Higher self-esteem!

Understand we have all been there and there is always a tendency to continue to say these things, but as your self-esteem grows, the needs lesson. Truthfully, it just feels good for someone to validate that you are ok as you are, but rare that an opinion isn't attached. When you hear that word "but"…shake it off the best you can. If it is all of the time…maybe you need to change your friends, your environment or set stronger boundaries. Maybe all three☺

We have been so conditioned by listening to people and their opinions all the way up through to political races. We become numb to what is being said because we doubt the truth from anyone. Our own end results seem to dictate truth even though we can't identify what the truth is actually. It affects you more deeply when it comes from someone you believe is your loyal friend or family member and you may spend your lifetime seeking that approval.

Do not link your success or failure to the opinion of others. If you did something that did not have positive results, express your feelings about it only if someone persists to needle you with a contrary remark, nip their comments in the bud and voice that everyone needs to let it go because you did. It is not their issue to deal with anyway. Learning lessons are a part of growth and maybe you are teaching them a lesson as well. It isn't always about us remember☺.

CHAPTER 18

A Path of Mistakes

Success does not consist in
never making mistakes,
but in never making the same
one a second time.
— GEORGE BERNARD SHAW

The past chapters are all linked with similar meaning and all with a common solution. Uncovering which aspect of drama you may be dealing with is a very fine line with similarities. I do not want you to become more fearful of taking risks to make a mistake because of all the dysfunctions that exist. There are no mistakes in life; only lessons. What this means is whenever something happens, no matter the outcome...learn from it, evaluate it and process other outcomes. If you can learn to accept mistakes, shortcomings, and unwanted events and people as opportunities, you will feel less stressed. Are you the perfectionist that allows for no mistakes?

We know there are those who refuse to accept they did anything wrong. It was someone else or it was the system that failed. This is known as a victim mentality. They rationalize, deny, make excuses, justify, and blame. These people have not yet learned to accept responsibility for creating the outcome or for their choice in maintaining an outcome they obviously are not happy about.

If you do something incorrectly, erroneously, or something that makes you feel guilty, you usually get furious with yourself more than others *unless you are a bit of a narcissist.* Most of us have a habit of beating ourselves up mentally over and over again. The fact is when you make a mistake; there is going to be a lesson to learn. Otherwise, you would have known the correct decision to make. No lesson needed. You usually know the correct answer first, but doubt yourself. Mistakes offer you the opportunity to explore an area where perhaps you are deficient, need additional knowledge, or need to re-evaluate your approach. If you even take the risk to make a mistake, you will eventually learn what you need to know to adjust future decisions.

Reflecting on past behavior and decisions is educational. Unrelenting remorse or guilt about past mistakes serves no useful purpose. Excessive guilt is one of the biggest destroyers of self-esteem, individuality, creativity and personal development. Self- condemnation about a previous wrong only increases the chance that you will make the same mistake again. Intense retaliation over wrongdoing may make you feel falsely absolved of guilt. This sense of absolution almost gives you permission to do the same thing all over again — illogical but true.

Let me share with you some of the most common "guilt triggers":

- Not always being there for your children, partner or parents.
- Saying "no" at work or at home.
- Taking time for yourself

You need to release the fear that if "I" do or don't do this, something will go wrong. If you educate yourself up front with information on a subject, you will obviously make a better decision or decide after reviewing the facts that the best decision is no decision. If you have little to lose by going with your gut and no added information is really necessary, then why not? I know people who have beginning remorse before they even make a decision. It takes them forever to finalize a purchase and they ruminate over the facts to the point they confuse themselves and nothing gets bought. They talk themselves out of the situation completely just because they get stuck in fear of making a mistake.

This fear of making mistakes will trigger stress, anxiety, and depression for taking a chance of any kind. Perfectionists perseverate and end up never trying anything because of potentially making that mistake and losing money on a regretful purchase. It is a horrible cycle. Perfectionism means do your best...not "perfect". It is not necessary for everyone to like you or to see you as perfectly competent / perfect in everything you do. If you make a mistake you are not a failure...some become embarrassed and become more perfectionistic which increase the stresses. This self-critical cycle will assassinate your esteem.

Procrastination and emotional paralysis have a shared quality of fear. We have been so mistreated by predatory parasites we become prisoners of our own doubts. We prefer taking no action because it might draw unwanted attention and therefore we freeze at the slightest uncomfortable crossroad. While frozen one can get caught up in their own polarized thoughts—one thought focused on disappointing someone by doing nothing and the other thought focused on distressing that same person by following through. Someone could even procrastinate as a way to save face. It's often easier to rationalize by saying, "I would have done better if I had more time."

Stalling for fear of making a mistake or appearing foolish causes an individual to panic and a possibly a good idea stays hidden. An employee may also become so focused on the details of the job that he or she becomes unable to complete a task. You have heard..."they can't see the forest for the trees". In the worst cases people just stop trying. In relationships they have high unachievable expectations. This can cause overly critical demands of other people so one looks smarter.

Some people feel being a perfectionist is a compliment. The problem is a perfectionist's belief can undermine an individual's self-esteem and wreak mayhem in relationships. Using a similar scenario from an earlier chapter: two people who achieve the same sales goal, but one does it faster than the other. Which person will feel better? The one that comments, "I did my best and achieved results," or the one that states, "I wonder what I did wrong–why is it taking me longer?" The one who overly criticizes his or her performance will feel worse.

Over time, this self-critical attitude will not only affect performance but the expectations for others to be perfect are also going to add to the stress. As the need to be and expect perfection increases, an individual's stress or anxiety level will also increase because the goal is impossible. The ability to perform mental tasks will decrease. Thus, attitudes that come from overly intense obsessions affect job performance, school performance, and even everyday tasks.

Although the degree of perfectionism may vary from mild traits that do not interrupt daily functioning to severe traits that cause complete dysfunction and paralysis. Both are still more common in the United States as media has portrayed perfection in their touched up and enchanting life of sales. We see commercials of women before and after a special cream is applied. We watch television programs in which the children are well behaved because of a certain toy or problems are resolved in 30 minutes with a new technology. We know about the print ads that use models with perfect bodies and attractive features. Wherever we turn, we are inundated with the message of perceived perfection. If we don't achieve these standards, we come to believe something is wrong with us. Our ego sucks it all up. Perfectionism adds to our anxiety and depression as the individual never achieves the standards he or she believes we are expected to meet.

First, it is important to give yourself permission to make mistakes. What stops you from self-endorsing your own present needs? Probably and most likely because we still hear our parents giving us permission over and over and we forget we are grown up now and don't need anyone's permission. Life does change and forever will change and this includes our needs and view of life. After you become aware of this historical need for approval, why does the "all or nothing" thinking continue to linger catastrophically? Obviously growing up, things were more black and white and understanding the gray area was difficult to teach a child. It was right or wrong, black or white, do it or not do it. Now seeing gray makes you feel hopeless because no one taught us there was a gray area. This often is notable by "what if" questions. All or nothing thinking can be categorized as opposites–good/bad, black/white, up/down—nothing in between. Therefore, a person either succeeds or fails; no lessons needed. Feeling hopeless occurs with the speculative belief a person already knows the outcome of an action or lack of action and there is no control over future events if we make changes. It either is or isn't. Therefore, there is no need to attempt changing the situation....paralysis of action.

The goal is to face and replace any belief that supplies more stress and dysfunction into your life. There may be a need to let go or withdraw from people or groups who keep feeding you concerns about making poor decisions because you need approval from them. They are trying to keep you dependent. Start experiencing mistakes by taking the opportunity to deliberately make them. One thing to remember is what one person may consider a mistake may not upset another person.

The important thing is taking a risk to overcome a fear and learn more than you can learn from just a book. Book learning is great but without allowing yourself to experience what you read will cause the fear to lay dormant and become an unwanted judgment or opinion which you cannot back up as truth for yourself.

I want to paraphrase someone I learned from... We all need reminded at intervals to re-ground ourselves and this also includes me:

... *"Realize that each individual is at the exact place they need to be. That friends and family may not perceive as you do, may not understand as you do, that this tremendous leap forward has occurred. Do not try to convince them, do not argue with them, for it is not perhaps their journey and they may sabotage yours. Instead, live your own life...focus on creating your inner reality and allow this process to be that which is your stance alone, your presentation to others. You do not need to debate others that you are correct, that there is something happening, for all are immersed in their own perspective reality. There is no need to teach those who are closed, those who are not teachable, but as you live your life you become the strong architect of your new reality. Those who have a capacity to learn and grow will see your truth will understand there is something different about your reality and how you manifest your reality. This is my goal to help assist you to your new reality if you are open and choose to change." A Cosmic Awareness* focus on creating your inner reality and allow this process to be that which is your stance, that which is your presentation to others. You do not need to debate others that you are correct, that there is something happening, for they are immersed in their perspectives of reality. That there is no need to try to teach those who are closed, those who are un teachable, but as you live your life, as you become a strong architect of your new reality, those who have within themselves a capacity to grow and learn will see your Truth, will understand there is something different about how you hold reality, how you manifest reality....this is my goal to help you bring about the new you ...CA/js

CHAPTER 19
Victim or Bully?

When people don't like themselves very much, they have to make up for it. The classic bully was actually a victim first.
— TOM HIDDLESTON

If you ever had questions to why you feel trapped, less than, unable to verbalize when you need to, unable to love, afraid to take risks, stay with learned dysfunction or caretaking others to the point you have nothing left to expend: I will identify some possible experiences you may have incurred that can lead to these low self-esteem, poor boundary, repeated dysfunctions... This always builds from childhood training when we are taught to feel like a victim of circumstance. Some of these childhood experiences that can lead to low self-esteem causing the encompassing traits above can include:

- being harshly criticized, abused, molested
- being yelled at, or beaten
- being ignored, ridiculed or teased, bullied
- being expected to be "perfect" all the time
- Living up to someone else's ideal
- experiencing failures over and over

Unfortunately many of us are conditioned to not feel our emotions especially after experiencing any of the above. We are taught that showing fear, anger and sadness can be bad or childish so we begin to repress without any known or taught release valve to handle the excessive buildups except go to our room and stew more about it. Emotions are part of being human. Not having a 'healthy' release of the emotions is a serious problem as we have mentioned. We can be unaware of this because victim thinking is engrained at that very impressionable age of black and white thinking.

This is a time we may feel incapable of protecting ourselves or getting our needs met. We have to rely on others and if they don't comply in a healthy, productive manner... we communicate messages to ourselves that we cannot possibly win...aka enters the helpless victim or victim turned bully depending what they mimic.

This oppressed energy pattern can also be passed down from generation to generation through "generational" repression so it can become very strong conditioning. An example we can still relate to is the unkindness to slaves which lingered through generations due to learned oppression of that race. We have talked about generational learning and how it creates baggage for us when we don't even realize this is encumbering our present issues. Don't we have enough to worry about without having Great Grandpa's problems still haunting us along with our own problems of the time?

It can be difficult to fully experience and release underlying emotions if one has become a victim. Just by telling yourself the truth of where you are and what you are feeling can begin to shift the victim energy. Just say I am feeling anger or whatever the emotion might be. Sometimes just getting angry and saying it can assist the anger to shift. When we hit on the right emotion, the intensity of the emotion can begin to loosen and the anxiety / tension will begin to go away. This we know isn't an overnight process and it will resurface again and again until the strength of its power has minimized to nothing. It may take some time to wear a new path through the woods especially if we have had emotional build up since childhood and beyond.

Once we shift from feeling like a victim then we can again experience the underlying natural emotions without intensity and eliminate the paralysis of never taking any risks to trust in ourselves or others ever again. If one feels or thinks they can't handle a situation or life in general then they are probably stuck in victim momentum. Feeling overwhelmed can be a sign of a victim. "Why do I always agree to take on more?" Needing approval again? The truth is everyone has the capacity to handle every situation in their life. "God won't give you any more than you can handle" but if you add what others expect then overload is possible.

Hopelessness is a lie either taught to us or we have convinced ourselves of its existence because of many let downs. We do not discern what is ours or what is theirs and the weight of it all is too much to handle. We also do not understand we need not accept the dysfunction of being a victim...most especially if the original situation occurred 50 years ago in someone else's lifetime and you are being loyal to the concept.

We know people are suffering difficult times in their lives right now. People wonder why bad things are happening to them. It is said very spiritual people sometimes have difficult lives because they have chosen to burn off a lot of karma, for those who believe in karma. Also much is learned about compassion by suffering through it yourself.

Often difficult situations offer us great opportunities for growth and learning. Sometimes when we get beat up by life; it can be a very humbling experience. Some of us learn the hard way. Some of us need tough things to happen to anchor our lessons more firmly. If we are open and willing to look at ourselves and experience the good with the not so good then I think the growth process can be much easier and fun. Look at it as your own personal adventure and journey. Emotions play an important role in good health so take control of yourself and your emotions. Learn to relax and accept calm if that is what is missing.

To step back for a minute, children who are bullied can become anxious, depressed and lonely with a higher risk of suicide. Children who bully are more likely to have had peer rejection, conduct issues, anxiety, academic difficulties, and engage in rule-breaking conduct. A substantial number of children have been victimized by bullying and yet have bullied others to complete the cycle. They all struggle to control their emotions of anger and frustration and, as I have said, no proper way has been taught to help them deal with these explosive uncontrolled outbursts or the reverse of holding it all inside.

Bullies feel fear, shame, embarrassment and guilt and they are smart enough to recognize they can use the same to weaken their target. Shame is an inside wound caused by embarrassment. It is a normal response and stems from actually knowing right and wrong from somewhere along the line. The target recipients of this shame may be quiet or shy with little confidence yet. Maybe they were sheltered too much or they too lived in an environment where they were told to be seen and not heard. Again, go to your room and allow it to magnify your feeling of embarrassment of not being "good enough".

Becoming aware is the first step for the shift in you. It is ok to say "I had no idea…this is the first I have experienced anything like this. I was taught being strong and toughening up was all normal." You will gain confidence little by little and will not be afraid of being shut down for what you feel and say. Express your disapproval while rational and in control of your thoughts. Letting it build up... well, you all don't need me to tell you the end result of that method. This is indeed difficult when it comes to family and friends as you have loyally surrounded yourself with the people that usually keep you stuck as a victim or bully. Hot buttons can be very strongly felt as everyone knows.

Know there is better around the corner after a safe release. How could it be worse unless you fall back into the same role? Take time to learn about yourself. Do not jump back into a relationship or you will be tested again without more information to help you. Stay aware and one day it will click. Do not beat yourself if you do fall into the same again. I have beaten myself up before and I am much more angry with myself; but I apparently didn't completely see all I needed to learn.

I was taught to be a do-gooder. Compulsive do-gooders are also afraid of or deny their own natural emotions of aggression and hostility by avoiding confrontation from the bully. They try always to do what is "best," preferring to be placating, submissive, or self-sacrificing rather than expressing or fighting for what they genuinely feel, lest they "make waves." I was taught you get more with honey than…. the nicer you are the better. Unfortunately many were taught like me to not react, move on and ignore it. It isn't right or wrong…just is…and now we have to make the effort to change this thinking or our own health goes awry.

So you see, it is learned, inherited and/or mimicked behavior which can be unlearned, thrown away and relearned. You can walk to the tune of your own drummer in a healthy manner that does not make your head want to explode. So if you don't understand what happened to you and why you cannot get it together…start from where you know, look around at who and what you were taught and decide if this is what you believe to be. If you don't know then start making those mistakes so you can begin to learn and create the future you can trust through your own experience. You do not need to hang onto it forever out of loyalty to the ones who taught it to you. If you can truly evaluate the truth of their lives, you will see the truth of why you may still be a victim or bully.

CHAPTER 20

Self Sabotage

"And there's also 'To him that hath shall be given.' After all, you must have a capacity to receive, or even omnipotence can't give. Perhaps your own passion temporarily destroys the capacity."

C.S. LEWIS

P eople who self-sabotage are afraid to receive. Self-sabotage is a slow progression that causes people to compete with their own thoughts and urges. Though we all make mistakes, a true self-saboteur continues to accelerate their bad decisions even after a life lesson opportunity. Addicts, for example, maintain excuses to the point of potential delusional thinking where they begin to believe their own lies; so to avoid doing, they substitute... Procrastination is part of this list. Why? Procrastination is the breach between intention and action and the person does not want to close that hole. It requires taking action and we already know that procrastination is easier. We therefore act out.

People have good intention to act, but when the time comes, instead of acting, they waiver in off-center reflections making all of the excuses to justify an unnecessary and potentially harmful delay. No one makes this decision but us... The self, in fact, sabotages its own intention.

You may have learned to 'do things on your own' in order to feel secure by yourself. It is a form of projecting rejection in some ways leaving those behind that never made time for you. Maybe you did not have anyone to guide you when you needed help or were turned down. There are parents who were just not emotionally present or maybe they ignored important needs for attention, affection and comfort. This can result in a sort of hidden isolation in every familiar relationship because being by yourself is something normal to you.

We have always heard that someone who self-sabotages will attract inattentive partners or compensate by over eating alone, spending or some other extreme behavior. One can fluctuate to the reverse trait and neglect basic needs. Again, the subliminal expectation turns out to be the norm and now becomes embedded in the subconscious where it is buried deeply within the personality. Now one does not even realize what the problem is or how it started. One sits and wonders how they got this way. It leads to self-punishment where one beats themselves up and manifests dysfunction by escaping or avoiding that which can't be identified.

The flip side of inattention is being smothered by a parent's consistent adoring attention that births a need for constant validation as we have stated. Maybe you were kept under a thumb of control keeping your experiences limited. Both result in your eventual reluctance to know your own needs. You get to the point of always feeling like never knowing what you want. You attract an overbearing partner who continues the same presentation of control incurred in your past because you feel safe again that someone is in control. Either way, you subtly flee in the opposite direction or directly back into the same because it feels safe. Self-sabotaging behavior results from a careless attempt to rescue ourselves.

At times, trying less brings faster results but we are conditioned that we must do something all the time. Being confused about what "that" is causes addictions to excel because undertaking "whatever that is" overwhelms us.   We have no real answer and keep repeating the same exitus at the eleventh hour. When we let go of the reins (or whoever is holding them) the universe is pleased to guide us if we listen. It may not appear exactly how we envisioned or in the exact form expected, but it always comes in its own good time and usually better than we hoped. A novel result will occur if there is flow instead of retreat. I found the result is always better than expected too.

At that 11th hour, we feel we have been swimming against one heck of a strong current!   We have pushed and pushed, done without, sacrificed everything and nothing seems to work.   We wear out, become pessimistic, give up and then mentally grow tired which is when those doubts slide right in.   Any other perceptively negative and demeaning comments by others layer themselves into your own doubts...maybe it is time to surrender and know you have done all you can do at this point. Take time to relax and re-charge in silence and listen. It is not to suggest that you should give up completely, but take a step back and keep goals in focus; have some fun away from the grind to recharge. It is absolutely necessary in this day and age and quite difficult when there are families and friends, etc. that won't leave you alone for a minute to think. You can see I have been there!

Breathe in silence and listen to your own mind; the answer always emerges if you don't fall short of waiting. Many times, our insistence on forcing the outcome gets in the way of the outcome that would be most beneficial to our *Self. (or someone throws you off by dictating your outcome)* When you let go, things often turn out exactly as they are meant. There is no need to run. We can all develop more patience and developing patience is just that.... developing a skill. We aren't born with it. We can start anytime to develop the perseverance we need for future adversity. As I have said I am still developing it☺ I always hope... *at least let me be able to enjoy my rewards before I get to old to enjoy it.* That is obviously not total patience yet☺

When the temperament range of anger, irritation, and blame becomes intense due to impatience, it becomes a form of self-sabotage when it turns into rage or an uncontrollable reaction. Rational conversation or thought is now hard to manage. It is difficult to not act on these urges of intense anger, irritation or blaming/shaming. Over-reacting can wear many masks when we become overwhelmed. Shop o'holics, neat nicks, video games vs. going outside, cutting on themselves, over exercising, gambling, sex, work, porn, food, substance use, and as I have said 'a way of life' can be the addiction and you don't even realize it. And yet we blame others for these self-sabotaging escapes.

People who have these addiction/obsessions do feel a veiled sense of anger at themselves and redirect this anger to parents for not guiding them in the right direction ... maybe they just follow the parent's footsteps because that is all they know to be valid whether it is same addiction or a different one. It is normal and the only release they know. Self-sabotage is ignoring growth and accepting a truth that is not valid for you. You are caught in the middle of two opposing worlds.

Low self-esteem is the birthplace of addictive self-sabotaging behavior. Addictions come in the usual disguises of alcohol and drugs to eating disorders, abuse or obsessive behaviors. Believe it or not, but depression and negativity can be an addiction and a lifestyle. As I have said before, we get comfortable being uncomfortable; our words and thoughts follow suit thereby creating results of the same nature.

These habits or ways of life become a problem when it seriously and negatively affects daily life and the people around us. We have a propensity to avoid what we don't like, so it can take time for a person to admit there is a problem and most often, the people closest to the individual are the first to recognize it. Understand it is not their responsibility to deal with you and your new "friend" or crutch, but feel blessed if they try. Do not let them enable you though. You can fix it. Do it before you crash and burn. We have an entire culture built around addiction and obsession and this is not nourishing to anyone involved.

We try to defend our unhealthy choices by saying no one understands what we have been through. No one needs to understand, but you need to face your choices. We want our way, to get ahead, to achieve, and to "look good." Blaming anyone who attempts to come between you and your methods for getting there usually becomes the target of your own impatience. We prefer a "comfortable" state of pain or pleasure whether rational or not because it is a familiar habit. Are you motivated by pain or pleasure? Both can push us to find solutions. The resolution to either is an internal job; not by blaming others or self sabotaging.

The eleventh hour is that last possible moment at which a choice may be needed. Problems or solutions appear depending on your choice☺. Usually fear of failure (or success) and/or a lack of energy can lead to a delay by dawdling again. People who drag their feet become frustrated and spin their wheels; the opposite type person may wear themselves out completely reaching for a goal impatiently; both taking a real toll on your self-esteem.

This creates troublesome problems .... like guilt, stress, anxiety and /or lack of motivation. Too much or too little can cause the same results for self-sabotage. You may be taking on too much and causing more stress and pressure on yourself. This clouds your judgment and causes those offensive negative emotions to explode. You may be missing simple solutions to problems because you're rushing so much you don't pay close enough attention to details thereby creating bigger problems. If you avoid taking responsibility for trying anything new that might enhance your dreams, you've become too attached to the old way. All will sabotage your visions of success.

CHAPTER 21

Social Media and Self Esteem

*Social media demands a lot of us on
top of our already demanding lives.
So let us disconnect long
enough to renew ourselves.*
SIMON MAINWARING

W e have discussed our thoughts and how
it affects our self-esteem. Social media
can also give us a false sense of belong-
ing. This makes it increasingly easy to lose one's
self to cyberspace connections. Not saying it is all
bad, just check yourself. If you watch the movie
"HER"…you will see what I am talking about by the
actor getting caught up in the cyber world of love
by having a relationship with the computer and in
the end that cannot be trusted as a source of comfort either. I am not going to dwell on this subject,

but I feel it is important to point out that computers are great and make life easier, but don't forget about the real world right in front of you. Do not forget to get your children out in the sunlight and with you by their side!

When we look to social media, we end up comparing ourselves to what we perceive is the norm which can lower our self-esteem if we do not meet those standards. On social media, everyone's life looks perfect, but you're only seeing a snapshot of reality. Yes, we can be whoever we want to be with social media and no one will ever know unless they visit you. If we view what we see literally then it's possible that we will feel we are falling short in life. Again, whose thoughts are we allowing to control us?

How do you tell if your social network habit is healthy or harmful? If you find yourself feeling stressed, anxious or having negative thoughts after using social media, it may be time for a break or if you are obsessed with reading and posting all of the time and it begins to affect your work and social life. I knew someone that was obsessed with the number of comments and likes she got from her posts on Facebook. She used to tell her boyfriend

WHERE IS MY MAGIC?

to post the same thing to see how many likes and comments he received. I think a bit too much? Plus it can be just rude.....it is so noticeable that people are buried in their phones while driving, standing in line, shopping, walking....I remember giving smoke breaks during my presentations and now it is cell phone breaks.

Self-concept is how you perceive and evaluate yourself. How can you evaluate yourself if you cannot lift your head up from the computer or phone? You can have a positive or a negative self-concept depending on how you allow others to poison your mind. Yes, some things may be motivating or trigger you to buy/do something which is ok, but when you get frustrated trying to achieve the image the media portrays it affects your Self-image and Self-worth which reflects the conditioning or how it makes you feel about yourself.

We listen to what others say to us and assume they are correct so now that perception (right or wrong) affects our beliefs, attitudes and opinions and therefore our decisions....and finally our self-esteem.... which is how you finally FEEL about yourself (emotional). So your Self-concept is developed through interactions / misinterpretations / perceptions of what is seemingly valid through other's eyes. How confusing can that be?

We know people can interpret the same exact sentence in many different ways. Allowing the social media, the TV media etc. to control your direction and thoughts will not enable you to find your own passion. You need to find what interpretation is you and only you can identify that in the end. Use the social media as a means to an end. Do not make it your only source of information that answers all your questions so you do not have to actually experience life in the real world.

I am appalled at the toy makers and video companies that create the videos with the real life violence. I mean, come on, where did they think this would lead? Not to date myself, but where are the Andy Griffith shows for our youngsters to watch in their formidable years? I still love to watch all of those shows because it calms my system down. Even the black and white is a nice break. So I appeal to the media to make an effort to change your shows, change your videos so people can actually re-charge by watching TV instead of being freaked out after they watch something so possibly real and violent.

The world of tech is here to stay, but it does not stimulate all of the senses...yet. Balance is the key and if you are fearful to let your kids go out...understandable...you will need to make an effort to be with them up to a certain age where you feel safe they can handle themselves. Even back in my day, my father was always with us for everything we did...boy and girl scouts, church outings, school trips. We used to think how strict he was and get upset, but my brothers and I are thankful looking back. There is effort as a parent, but you are the guides to everyone's future. The world didn't get this way by itself. I am not going to dwell on this topic but I do feel it is a layer we need to consider.

CHAPTER 22

Learning to Trust Again

Trust in what YOU love, continue to do it,
and it will take you where you need to go.
NATALIE GOLDBERG

As I have eluded in my beginning chapters and books, we have much to contend with that is not even ours. There's a lot of pressure in life. Too much really! Just working and earning enough money to live is difficult, but trying to find our purpose, passion and true love can add to an already unsettled and confused state of mind.

Small percentages of people from an early age know exactly what kind of career they want (or maybe they were pushed into a certain career by a parent living out their dream). Most of us do not even feel that lucky because our parents paid no attention to what abilities we excelled in growing up.

There was no guidance, so we have been muddling around trying to find our niche. We may roughly know what we want or what we think we want by observing or listening to others. We may experience what "that" is all about and decide '*no way*' which is ok too. It is a start. For those in that boat, the desire for that "something" seems to change a lot and as you get older, you start to get frustrated. I felt frustration for many years because I knew I was good at anything I tried, but it seemed master of nothing. I used to compare myself to others so trust in me was elusive. I was so busy asking myself if I could do what they were doing instead of what I wanted to do. So how can you trust in yourself, if you have no real direction?

I just want to say you will get there if you listen to yourself and observe your own abilities. I can look back and see how everything I tried was a piece of my puzzle whether I made the decision on my own or someone else made it for me. The difference in finding "it" is... if you give up and accept the "what is". Your attitude while on the journey makes the big difference. I never gave up, I never thought I was forever doomed, I looked at everything as a layer of learning, good or bad and kept plowing forward, hitting walls ALL of the time. I got depressed, sad, exhausted, angry, and isolative thinking I would never find my niche. So when you are already kicking yourself and then have family and friends telling you what you should be doing, your trust in life goes by the way side. I believe, now, I have found the direction and yet I know there is more to this direction open for me. I have no idea where I am being led to this day. That takes the magic out of it!

Feel good about where you are and make the next step one YOU want and then learn as much as you can. That direction may work for only awhile and another one appears whether by your choice or someone else's decision. As long as you are making your own decisions based on what you want and need, you are on your path. If the path changes suddenly, thank the last path, let it go, and move on. Do not waste your energy blaming others if it doesn't work.

Everyone tends to struggle against themselves because of the inability to slow down and trust. Our intuition lays dormant ready to be released when we relax enough to hear it, and yet we falter because we get caught up not only in our fears and doubts but everyone else's. This is the struggle.

Maintain your determination and your faith that you *can* keep persevering. Look at past fears and doubts; the part you felt unable to change, at the time. Did you make it through? Was it as bad as you envisioned? Sometimes new opportunities will come from unexpected occurrences that change your direction as stated in Chapter 1. You have a choice to follow or not; whether it results in good or bad isn't the issue unless you don't learn from it. Sometimes these diversions could not have been anticipated with your rational mind. Maybe the opportunity is so different than the path you originally chose, but if it feels right, why not try it? It could be the layer you need to complete the original project you were working on or the diversion you need if you are blocked. Hindsight would not be necessary if you trust in the beginning. We always have hindsight though as a backup to our future choices.

Learning to trust again after being betrayed by someone or some event you counted on is difficult. You know that trust is elemental for forgiveness and healing of yourself. It is essential for you to be able to move on and dispense with the sting that hangs around like that annoying bee. It is important for healthy self-esteem not to hold onto resentment.

Resentment will literally get into your crawl (intestines) and start becoming a real physical ailment even to point of cancer as I have and will talk about in other chapters.

Trust involves risk, and re-trusting sometimes with the same people who betrayed you in the first place involves even greater risk. It means putting yourself "out there" again, toughening up your boundaries, expressing your disappointment if they do betray or did betray you. You always have the choice to tolerate and allow someone back into your life. Everything is a test of sorts but know you do not need to let them back in. Maybe it is obviously finished business. You know that you know it will not work. You feel it strongly. If you do let them back in and nothing changes on their part or yours, liberate yourself from the situation but don't beat yourself up for trusting again. We all want so deeply to trust in others before ourselves and maybe we need another dose to make the original decision valid. Trust in ourselves first.

My guess is you will be more aware of making the same decision over. *"First time, shame on you, second time, shame on me."* This statement makes you want to beat yourself up if you give someone a second chance and you find out it is worse than the first time. I have been there and done that! It happens. Apparently I or anyone needs more to learn from this situation, so flow with it, make new decisions and stick by those decisions. If your need is attention and validation from others, which we have talked about, trusting in yourself to handle it differently will be so much more difficult. It creates a whole new set of problems.

When a person is not able to get noticed and needs to be substantiated, he or she will act out by saying or doing something that creates drama. Attention is attention whether good or bad. They will make stinging comments or create a problem to get a reaction (Push the buttons). Jealousy could rear its head. Once in a while is not a problem until it becomes a lifestyle and exhausting people on the other end. It keeps you off balance. Do you know anyone who is in or creates constant commotion? You find you want to avoid them or not answer the phone just so you don't have to hear it all over again.

It is difficult to endear yourself to someone that wastes your time and their own on a continuous basis. We struggle with ourselves every day to accept others for who they are because we want to accept with flaws included. BUT, we do not need to tolerate the effect it has on us. If it disturbs what we are trying to accomplish and puts doubt in our own heads to ignore our own needs with the directions we have chosen, it may not be worth having them around. If they cannot understand this, it is their problem, not yours. Trust your body to tell you what to do.

Being betrayed by those we expected to be trustworthy and reliable causes confusion about when / who to trust once you realize they were the ones who faulted you. We may be so needy for acceptance we trust any person who simply appears nice or shows what seems to be unconditional attention. There actually may be a hidden agenda you won't see until too late and usually in their favor; as they sense and use our kind hearted, vulnerable, easily taken advantage of and easily manipulated needs as by the narcissist. It may be a person who just consistently needs attention and validation that keeps you off balance with no intended malice which in turn weakens your ability to stay on your focus. You are constantly getting sucked into their diversionary tactics either way.

If we allow the façade of their false confidence to infiltrate our true trusting nature, it drains our energy to the point we begin to doubt our ability to make or trust in those decisions ever again. As I have said before, when we are tired, the doubts start shadowing again. They have you where they want you now by creating the constant drama and diversions to fulfill their neediness. You start to isolate and build a wall of protection that takes a bulldozer to knock down. Maybe this is the best way to re-charge, but allowing them to win by not having the strength to make a decision for yourself anymore means your boundaries need more work or you need to get away from them!

As time passes, patterns will evolve, and only then can we really know who another person is and their true ethics. So give your new connections time before you give all away to them. Being with someone who continually makes you feel wrong, guilty, or not good enough is not going to make you happy obviously, so why torture yourself by trying to get validation from them. If you seek the attention anyway, your self-esteem may again need some fine tuning.

It is so much easier to trust in your Self first and foremost. Any successful interpersonal relationship needs a feeling of connectedness and trust from both sides. Trust creates healthy wholeness. You may have doubts you are going to attract someone who is whole. Try evaluating people who also believe in themselves first and the rest will fall into place accordingly. Take your time to see if concerning patterns evolve after the masks fall off. And the masks WILL fall off eventually. We have to kiss a few frogs to find our prince/ess even if it is platonic friendship. The prince/esses are few and far between it seems, but they are out there.

We need to start questioning our decisions and what we accept for the sake of just having. The ability to trust in our choices affects our total self-esteem and equally to the degree that we rely on "defense mechanisms" to create the whole. The less trust we have, the more we rely on using defense mechanisms. *(Ex: Protecting our own faulty self-concept could exacerbate lying, cheating, drinking etc.)* Our ability to trust greatly affects our ability to "survive" in a healthy way. If you do not trust your decisions then step back and review. It only means you need something you haven't fulfilled in yourself. Once that is honestly defined, you won't need that person for anything ...you can enjoy their company with no strings attached. If they are tying you up in strings...get the scissors☺

CHAPTER 23

Flow of Material Abundance

I graciously allow and accept
abundance in my life...

L et us move on to another subject. Money is usually considered to be associated with power and wealth and some have the attitude that anyone with money has stepped on others to get it. This is one of the main reasons why the flow of material abundance has become a block for many of us. Money is actually blameless. Money offers opportunities and there is nothing wrong with that. With money you are able to create all of the things you desire. If you can accept and receive it with the correct attitude, you will expand the flow of money for both yourself and others. So, don't be afraid to receive money! I talked in earlier chapters about identifying your beliefs!

Money can come in many forms the same as opportunities as stated in my first chapter...free dinner from someone, rebate when you least expect it, kind gesture from someone or even a 2 for 1 dinner. Be grateful for everything that comes to you and more will come. If you dismiss the value of the "gift" whatever the amount or means in which it comes, you block that flow of energy for more to come. This is easier said than done because we have a tendency to dismiss something and pass right on by without being grateful. This requires a conscious effort as we equate money as tangible cash in hand.

As we live our lives we come upon situations that inspire us to imagine or dream of something that lies beyond our present conditions. Often this comes about from experiencing the opposite of what we want. When there is a contrast between what we want and what seems to be accessible, a desire is produced. This desire summons different energies into play which is all part of the universal energy.

The colors you surround yourself with can even assist you as we will discuss later. Keep the color green around for abundance even if it is a flower/plant. You will know what you need through your intuitional insights and type of abundance you are seeking. Color can keep your sense of flow intact, not actually bring money or other abundance to you☺. I do want to make clear; you still need to make effort and identify the abundance you seek.

If you hear yourself saying "I'm sick of never having any money" or "dread your bills coming in"…you know you have a block and your thoughts are leaning to lack instead of abundance. People don't get very far in life because they are constantly telling themselves they are not capable of making more or only if they had more money they could get what they want. Again this is a play on your own words. Everything you say or think is what is. We compare ourselves to others and keep ourselves in the "less than" mode of life.

We go through life thinking, real or imagined that we have been shorted somehow. Either our parents did not have any money to pass on or it slips through our fingers somehow when we do get it because we have had lack for so long. Maybe we spend all of it as soon as we get a windfall. And for what? Things we really don't need? We all have weaknesses, so how we process acceptance of receiving when we do get a "gift" will direct how we think about ourselves. Maybe someone while growing up pointed out the shortcoming of struggling for everything and it stuck to you. An example would be if someone said you will never be worth anything or you will never make anything of yourself. Maybe you were in a relationship where the spouse kept telling you that you were fat or incapable of having a thought in your head. This is a form of abuse of course, but when you hear it every day, it really sticks and grows tentacles.

Believing all of the inferior comments that come our way affects the incoming abundance that continues to miss us in whatever form it comes. Again this manifests as a self-esteem issue. This flow of energy does have an opposite swing to it though.

You can also hold on too tightly and the receiving end will also choke. Are you doing without or become so stingy you squeak? Know anyone like that? We have needs and yet we do without for fear of *not having* if we let go. You may have convinced yourself at some point you really don't need anything so you give to someone else "in need" who shows no gratitude for your sacrifice. You feel resentment because you didn't feel you really had it to give and now you do need something and can't get the money back; Some people make no effort to repay and when you are tight they still have the gumption to ask for more. Unfortunately, we have created this scenario as well.

...but doing for others *when we don't have it to give* may be enabling them and destroying ourselves in the end. We work hard and struggle to save only to have it leave us because of the incongruity of helping others at any expense. Are they truly doing anything to help themselves and /or is there a pattern you have yet to see from their taking? Are you so desperate for being accepted that you will place yourself in a financial crisis just to feel like you rescued someone? Maybe they needed to learn a lesson at that time *'by not having'* and you have now opened yourself up to being a source of rescue with no lesson learned except *what works without working for it.* Now enters your negative thinking about struggling and living on the pity pot of regret. Look what I have done for others! Holding onto resentment will create a block in your intestinal area which will eventually affect the health in this area. If you cannot truly afford to lose it, then don't give it away.

Enabling others for love is not love. Being afraid of economic loss by lost savings or jobs only indulges your fears about this. If you complain about how much everything costs or you could lose your job because of the economy... will keep you at bay from receiving more. Accept the good with the bad and move on whether it is financial or spiritual. Do not hold onto lack where you will manifest an even worse situation. Lessons learned hopefully and move on. Those toxic people will eventually fall away if you plug the hole and let go without resentment. It is what it is. Past. As I have said before, you can forgive yourself and them, but it does not mean you need to continue to tolerate the same behavior over and over.

I found this to be a missing piece for me as a rescuer. I played this learned mantra over and over as I developed ... "forgive and forget"...it just never made sense to me. If someone has betrayed me or used me in any way, how do I forgive them and I certainly will never forget it! I spent years tossing this around and at some point I realized we can forgive them and ourselves because everyone only does what they know to do at the time. Forgetting? I know realistically I will never forget and I don't need to forget! It is part of my developing pearl. Realizing this begins the shift and automatically changes my energy if I learn and never allow it to

ever happen again. If I fail the test a second time...
apparently I did not learn the lesson enough. We
are always tested. The test will come from many
different faces masked with similar hidden intent.
Some have refined their mask of intent and for you
to take the time to remember and discern your future decisions about a similar rescue are only in
your best interests in the end. Boundaries, dear
ones, and realizing everyone needs to deal with
their own creations of good or bad... we did it to
ourselves.

I repeat, the flow of abundance does not solely
mean *money*. It encompasses everything working
in sync. Your spiritual and physical abundance
will have an effect on the material abundance. It
all follows the same process. If you feel and think
you are poor. You are poor. If you think you are
overweight, you are overweight. If you are always
blaming others, you will stay in the pit of despair.
Watch what you say, think and believe. There is
magic in believing. You can choose whether you
make it positive or negative. We know the magic of
negativity works☹

CHAPTER 24

The Magic of Effort

*Continuous effort – not strength
or intelligence – is the key to
unlocking our potential!*
WINSTON CHURCHILL

We are barraged daily with all the manipulation, destruction and disease that are continuously growing on our planet. Many people and especially our youngsters are losing hope and wondering what is the purpose of life. Why should they keep on the struggle? The Law of Happiness tells you not to believe anything, but to question, explore, doubt and discover for yourself what your truth is right now. The biggest issue I see right now is people feel entitled to receive without effort and yet they sit on their backside and whine that they have nothing and there is no God. Their thinking process has become fragmented on how to achieve the wealth of the universe.

There are so many things we take for granted that come from the universe. We have education at our fingertips and an endless number of adventures to sample daily if we open our eyes and dig our faces out of the computer screens. We can change our looks, tastes and desires at any moment. We can experience nature in so many different ways and this includes experiencing all in silence either physically or virtually. What is the reason we limit ourselves or close ourselves off from these resources? It is usually out of fear, greed, or impatience to have and what the universe does offer us for free we take for granted. Do we take the people around us for granted as well?

Everything and everybody is a gift from the universe. Our skills, our knowledge and our capacity to understand how all enmeshes together is an amazing feat in itself that humans have over plant and animal. Yes, we assume or take for granted that all we have comes from school, parents, friends, strangers, TV, radio, etc…and it does….but in the end it all comes from universe.

We live in these limited shells designed by us. We can choose to be detached from the world using our perceived restricted capacities or we can open the door and let the reality of abundance flow right into our presence. It is said... "It is all there, all that we need, for the asking". Think expansively about the infinite potentials that life offers. Dream the dreams and exercise the capacity of your mind and emotions to embrace the wider opportunities. What stops it?

I know one reason is some parents are purging the imaginations of children by refusing to let them believe in fairies, Santa Claus or the Easter Bunny to name a few. We stunt their imaginations and ability to visualize at an early age. We also pray, we try to do the right thing, we do for others and yet here we sit with what appears to be nothing while all of the so called oppressors are getting the rewards. Remember the meek will inherit the earth. This is a fact and coming soon! Do not lose hope and know that the struggles we have all endured will be coming to an end if we stop the struggle within!

From a known silent and revered source of mine, it is quoted... *"The ones who think they are winning* *(because after all it's a game to them) are actually losing, they are creating their own destruction, and as they try to cling to power, like a cancer, they are now starting to devour their own. The ones who think they are losing (i.e. the ones most affected by the system in a negative way, which are the majority of the population) are actually **Winning!** The Creator has a "brilliant" sense of humor! He said to remember the quote "The meek shall inherit the Earth". Cosmic Awareness* It's up To YOU! All it takes is a simple shift in your thinking! It is that simple. Which path do you prefer to follow? You are at the crossroads but know in your heart, the correct direction to the wealth of the universe is gratitude.

Everyone is scrambling to find the "Secret" to having and not having. There are many books / videos out there that claim how simple it is. Just believe. This is true, but I think they are leaving out a few parts as that chef who won't tell the secret ingredient to make it work for you. We try and fail. May be I can help fill in a few gaps for you.

Setting goals for what you want would appear simple. I want more money, house, a new car and a second vacation home. Are these goals specifically clear and/or do they clash with each other as far

WHERE IS MY MAGIC?

as which one has as the strongest desire? A young woman may want to earn more money but also want to spend more time doing what her boyfriend wants in order to keep him happy. You need to make up your own mind and then put your energy into one or the other. Identify what direction you really want and aspire to and feel the drive to attain it. If you allow others to interrupt your flow or split requests into opposite directions, the result may not manifest the way you want. They flow with you or not.

We can want something a lot, but other emotions that need attention may interfere. People will try and tell you that a relationship is more important or they will complain you never do anything other than work. Yes you do need a balance, but do it on your own terms. You should feel the enthusiasm of attaining it. Try and remember the things you have accomplished in the past and what it took to achieve it. You need the faith and conviction that you can achieve it and want it so passionately that you can override the interruptions and obstacles that arise to stop you. You must want it for the higher good and maintain integrity and the power of effort to attempt achievement. You need to be flexible and listen to your inner voice to know when to rest and when to continue on. Have faith in your decision. "The greater your faith in your passion, the greater your accomplishments".

Do not hesitate to want material things or feel guilty for wanting it. The wealth of the universe will pick up your hesitation and delay your results until you are sure. The material world – our physical bodies and our desired personal situations are the groundwork for all our higher pursuits. Having harmony and contentment in your own life is the first step to your spiritual abundance.

I was taught not to disclose your goals to others until completed because it leaves you vulnerable to attacks from others. Silently move toward your goals until you achieve them. As they say, don't talk about it, just do it. People feel the need to talk about it because it makes them feel self-important. The less you say the better. Arrogance will stop the accomplishment from materializing. Do not be impatient about when it will happen. Easier said than done, I know. Impatience or confusion will postpone results. I can attest to this myself. Even though I felt I had been patient for years, I began to feel more impatient as I get closer. I finally surrendered if for no other reason than exhaustion.

At that point, I felt if it is meant to happen it will. The Divine has a plan for me and if this isn't the direction, I have done all I can do and no more with this intended plan of mine.

Impatience is a sign that you are worrying or doubtful it will come. Be certain of your faith in achieving the results and do not have expectations. Expectations mean you are waiting and waiting for that one thing to happen, but this also delays results. Isn't it when you surrender after all your hard efforts that something happens? You can relate to women trying to get pregnant and when they stop trying, it happens! Enjoy the process and know that it will happen. Follow your regimens of making it happen and don't focus or worry about the result.

Believe you have all the time in the world and then just take it one day at a time. Stay positive in every way with yourself. You are not compromising your feel good for anyone. Stay focused on what needs to happen and leave frustration at the door. Wishing for it will not make it happen without effort. You are the extension of the Divine and the effort you take to do the particulars necessary will make it easier for the Divine to make it happen for you. The amount of effort you make will equal the maximum amount of result the Divine can give you. As stated by the same mentor, "*You* are the arms and legs of the Divine; *you* are the feet and hands of the Divine. CA The Divine suggests the implication being your higher power is not able to walk, lift, handle things, or move around in an animated manner the way the human body moves around, except through its creation in the form of bodies that have arms and legs". Makes perfect sense to me!

I found that keeping my energy level up during this process was very difficult. Working 40 hours, running errands after work, trying to slip in some exercise and then spending weekends working on the books was exhaustive. I had people interrupting me, getting upset with me because I wasn't available for phone calls and/or visiting with them. I was beginning to pray for the cabin on top of the mountain. (*Haven't got it yet...lol*). You need energy to accomplish the result as well. The one thing that kept my energy level high was the desire to make it all happen...the process became obsessive when I started. I had to become frugal with my time, energy and money. I released as much wasteful energy as I could. As I write this book, I only pray/ask for the energy to complete what I need to for now. This book.

CHAPTER 25
The Magic of Emotion

All emotions are pure which
gather you and lift you up:
The emotion is impure which seizes only
one side of your being and so distorts you
RAINER MARIA RILKE

I think we can finally assert that all our major organs and bodily systems are affected by the amount of stress flow, *or not,* through our bodies. Each organ has a connected emotion and when there is an intense imbalance of this emotion, it can affect the organ's function. The flow of blood will be over-involved and work harder. This lack of flow will enhance problems. I mentioned earlier that I had a dull ache in lower back from an injury that acupuncture eliminated in one session. I was told the body was now protecting this injured area and creating an impasse of blood flow to other parts of my body causing the ache. This was also affecting my liver and making it work harder as well. Made sense to me and I was thrilled to have the pain leave when the impasse started flowing again. My liver tests were better too.

Another example: if you are depressed or worried, you can hinder the flow of energy within digestive meridians. If the energy flow blocks up, it can eventually be a precursor to more illness and disease in digestive organs. Eventually over time, worry and depression will cause a broader range of physical symptoms, such as:

- nausea and/or vomiting
- reduced appetite and weight loss or over-eating and weight gain
- belching and reflux
- abdominal distention
- constipation or diarrhea

Here are some other examples of parallel organ vs. emotion:

- You feel anger at a situation (liver)
- You feel sadness because you can't take your family somewhere nice (lungs)
- You worry because your family is also sad, mad and unhappy (spleen)

- You are stressed and anxious because the success or failure of this huge project falls on your shoulders (heart)
- The anger, grief, sadness and anxiety causes energy blockage or stagnation in the liver, lungs, spleen and heart.
- The organs thus accumulate heat and dampness or cold and dryness. They lose homeostasis or balance.
- The organs fail to move the energy as they should
- The organs fail to function properly
- Bacteria, virus, fungus grow in one or more of these organs.
- You develop digestion issues, breathing issues or blood pressure issues
- Illness ensues…the area your emotions keep pounding on will become your weak spot.

Chart is from:
http://www.qigongbyquist.com/blog/
emotions-can-affect-the-flow-of-qi-in-our-bodies

Emotion	Organs Affected with this Emotion	What Symptoms You will Have if the Emotion is Not Resolved
Grief, Anxiety	Primary: Lung, Large Intestine Secondary: Skin, dryness	Coughs, shortness of breath, asthma, bronchitis and pneumonia, dry skin, thin skin, fatigue, breathlessness, crying, weakness, and a feeling of tightness or oppression in the chest.
Mania / Stress (extended state of joy, laughter, over-excitement or agitation)	Primary: Heart/Pericardium, head, Small Intestines Secondary: Arteries, Veins, Tongue, Sweat	Heart palpitations, anxiety, insomnia, confusion, mental illness.
Worry / Depression	Primary: Spleen, Stomach, Pancreas Secondary: Muscles	Nausea and/or vomiting, reduced appetite and weight loss, over-eating and weight gain, belching and reflux, abdominal distention, constipation or diarrhea, tiredness, chronic fatigue, difficulty concentrating
Anger	Primary: Liver, Gallbladder Secondary: Tendons, Eyes	Headaches, dizziness, blurred vision, red eyes, confusion, tinnitus, high blood pressure.
Fear	Primary: Kidney, Bladder, reproductive organs Secondary: Bones, Ears	Frequent urination, bladder infections, incontinence, or bedwetting

Sorrow also damages the lungs. During pro-
longed times of sorrow or grief, breath and blood
flow are constricted, unable to flow easily in and
out of the lungs. It can exacerbate asthma and
other bronchial conditions of the lungs, such as
coughing, shortness of breath, bronchitis, etc. The
lungs are also affected by grief as demonstrated by
the heaving that occurs with crying. Grief depress-
es and weakens the lungs. However, this does not
mean that we should suppress sorrow or grief. It
is not healthy to withhold the emotion in response

to an upsetting event. Allow it to flow through you as it occurs.

Fear causes pain and disease in the kidneys, adrenals, and lower back and creates favorable conditions for urinary tract disorders and incontinence. The circulation of blood and breath slows down, resulting in conditions of excess and stagnation. A common sign of this is cold hands and feet. One is literally "frozen with fear." Chronic fear can lead to a host of debilitating conditions. If we do not have time to rest and regenerate our supply, our ability to cope with stress is impaired. If stress is constant, the body may forget how to re-turn to the healthy state, losing its ability to defend effectively to repair and heal damage.

The kidneys and adrenals also control brain function, especially memory. Scientific research has confirmed that fear and stress can weaken memory and create learning disabilities. Anger weakens the liver. This leads to muscular tension and various liver ailments, such as headaches, eyestrain, hemorrhoids, and irregular menstruation. The spleen is damaged by pensiveness. Pensiveness means excess concentration or an obsessive preoccupation with a concept or subject. Needless to say, college students often suffer from spleen-related disorders: gastric disturbances, elevated blood pressure, weakened immunity, and a tendency toward phlegm and colds. Maybe we think too much! Excess sympathy also harms the spleen. You enable the feeling of sadness or grief by allowing it to continue either by you or someone else who has had a significant loss.

Expressing normal adverse feelings is good for your health if moderated and not out of control. Rage will become violent to your insides. This kind of anger does not end after it explodes; without doubt that trail of resentment, frustration, and guilt will follow impeding good physical health. Studies have found the inability to express healthy anger and other emotions with no healthy release valve may suppress the immune system and create favorable conditions for the development of cancer.

So, how do we deal with the emotions? Understand they are ok and normal. They are not sinful or bad and you are also not inferior for feeling them. The emotions are natural…it is how you handle those emotions and if you have a healthy release of the emotion when overloaded. Notice what emotion is "acting out" and then own it as real and feel it! This will inhibit the trail of harmful / vibrating energy by keeping it loose and free flowing so as not to get stuck and stored up in the body as a blockage.

Remember, if one of the emotions erupts at an inopportune time and the emotion increases in intensity, relax and find a protected place to replay and process the emotion back into rational balance. Give yourself the time, breathe and accept that the irritation is coming from inside you.

There are certain physical feelings which are signs of repressing an emotion. Anxiety and frustration point to repressing fear or other emotions. Anxiety / frustration are not emotions but a physical resistance to feeling the emotion. They act like a lid on a pressure cooker keeping the emotions from surfacing. Ask yourself what emotion you are repressing / resisting and then verbalize to yourself that you are feeling that emotion. There may be a combination of emotions at this point, so dig until you find the original emotion that spearheaded the rest.

When we arrive at the correct initial emotion, that emotion can begin to relax and the anxiety will begin to wash away. When we start doing this it can take some time to identify the original emotion because we may have spent years repressing it and the flurry of other emotions have become a mask to protect!

Some incredible soul "openings" happen with people who are going through difficult situations. Many people who face the possibility of losing their lives can begin to face what is really important to them. They can really get in the moment because death can be right around the corner. Their hearts open, the masks disappear and they can live more realistic lives. Value judging is gone, resentment is gone and guilt is gone because they can now see that unconditional love for all is pure and peaceful. The heart likes peace and quiet just like the feeling of being in nature. So if you are having a challenging time you may just be in the process of creating your pearl. Learning to still feel joy, passion, integrity, kindness, dignity and love despite irritations which are a part of life will actually heal you from the inside out.

I believe that we are going through an incredible time in history that so many ancient traditions have spoken about for thousands of years. There are countless historical teachings coming to help us with our journey. There is tremendous light at the end of the tunnel! There are so many people who are forerunning their knowledge for you to grab onto and fly. I am only giving you a small piece of many things to help you to start thinking differently. I may have repeated myself, but everything interrelates and the repetition will help anchor for all for you.

CHAPTER 26

The Magic of Color

*The soul becomes dyed with
the color of its thoughts.*
MARCUS AURELIUS

C olor therapy is a means of using color in an attempt to affect our mood, emotions and possibly even our health. I do not profess, again, to be an expert on using color. I have included a website that I feel describes the parallels most succinctly, but you may need to do your own research if it is something that rings exciting for you. It can be fun as well as assist you in healing. As the website explains, you can use colored oils, colored lights directly on certain parts of your body to assist with healing. You can even use colored therapy glasses that can cause a shift in your eye spectrum.

Living in total obscurity without any enlightenment would obviously affect our mood. Think of the 'lack of color' and drabness of prisons and the weird sensation you get when you enter a prison. Remember how you feel after 3 weeks or more of rain or gloom and the sun finally comes out. Light is prismatic of color and healthy for us because all of the colors are present. There are so many links to identify what colors work best on certain parts of body. I only want to tantalize your thoughts!

I do not want someone to think this is a replacement for seeing a doctor, but combining all of the resources we know about can certainly assist the other in some way even if it is to prolong serious issues from reaching full prospective diagnosed ends. Anyone familiar with Chakras knows each color has a relationship with each other and when there is an energy block or illness, the color balance is off.

It is thought by some that our tissues and organs need these same colors as each has its own vibration. When disease, caused by stress or injury, disturbs an organ or part of your body, applying the associated color frequency can restore the body to health. Eastern medical practice teaches that we have meridians which carry energy through the body and connect to each organ as is used in acupuncture. This is the theory behind acupuncture which attempts to remove blockages to the energy flow. I have used acupuncture for pain and I found it helped immediately. I mentioned I had a dull ache in my lower back due to an injury and I thought that ache was going to exist forever. One acupuncture session handled it! Gone was the pain!

Color does not heal. Rather, it assists the body to heal itself and keep the energy of our mind and body flowing and in balance. Color therapy has been around since the ancient Egyptians, Greeks and the Chinese also used color to treat ailments. We do not want you to run out and over supply yourself in one color because understand that too much of something is also not good as with anything we do.

I will summarize some of what colors are thought to do and as I said you can research for yourself. This website listed has much to offer in information. (http://www.therapycolor.com/) Just to wet your palate for now:

RED: Stimulates alertness and excites. Affects more physically. It can be used to overcome negative thoughts, create a sense of self confidence. Too much can cause impatience and even aggressiveness. Certainly not a color for prisons☺ Base chakra.

ORANGE: Warm and joyful and affects more emotionally. Can create resourcefulness and happiness. Optimistic and remove inhibitions keeping you calm. Too much can cause frustration and you tend to eat more. Sacral area chakra.

YELLOW: Is warm and connects more to mental. It supports self-esteem and gaining knowledge. Good for decision making, more concentration and discernment. Too much can make you superficial and/or hyperactive. Solar plexus area chakra.

GREEN: Is a Master color. Refreshing and cool and connects to unconditional love. It precipitates peace, hope and balance. Growth and life *as in plants*. Causes calm and relaxation. Too much causes laziness. Heart area chakra. Promotes money thoughts☺

AQUA: Is cooling and connects to expressions. Soothing and openness can be created where you feel more freedom of expression. It can help with sleep. Too much is unknown☺

BLUE: Cold and acidic. You have more holistic thoughts. Helps with communication and creativity. It relaxes and calms hyperactivity. Too much can cause fatigue, insecurity and depression. Throat area chakra.

INDIGO: Cool and calming to nervous system. Serenity, imagination and better understanding of things. Greater intuition, higher intuition and better perceptions. Too much ...depression and feeling more separate from others. Brow area chakra.

VIOLET: Cools and connects to spiritual. Inspiring. Generosity and selflessness and suppressed appetite. Too much suppresses emotions and can cause insecurity. Crown chakra area.

MAGENTA: Balancing and connects to devotional love. Gentle. Peace. Too much can cause one to be too relaxed and promote more depression. Not good for chronically depressed or introverts.

PINK: Stress relief and calming aggression. Can be an appetite suppressant. Too much of pink is unknown as a deficient.

I understand the main areas in which color therapy has proved successful are those that involve mood, emotion and some aspects of mental performance.

However, advocates of the therapy claim that it can be used to assist healing in a variety of conditions, including the following:

Allergies
Anemia
Anxiety
Arthritis
Asthma
Depression
High Blood Pressure
HIV and AIDS
Hyperactivity
Insomnia
Low Blood Pressure
Migraine
Nausea and Vomiting
Neuralgia
Obsession

Stress... *to mention a few and certainly not limited to these.*

I have not personally used color directly on or in my body but have bought flowers and painted rooms per my mood desire and I know the chosen colors assisted, as stated above, in balancing what I needed balanced. If you correlate the chakra area per the color related to that chakra you can probably evaluate what color you need for what too.

True and complete healing occurs when the cause of the condition or illness is addressed. If recovery goes no further than a masking of the symptoms, then, eventually, that which brought about the need for healing will resurface in one form or another and all will seem useless. This is why I say use all avenues available and find the doctors that can direct you. I believe we all have the ability to heal ourselves, but I don't think we are all ready for that task yet. Much work needs to happen internally to get the self-esteem levels higher and higher for all of this to work. It can happen. Energy (spiritual) healers enhance their healing work with color healing. As they lay their hands on the patient, they mentally direct specific color rays into the patient's aura and body.

So have fun with color but not in too big of doses! I have seen bedrooms that are completely purple...waaay too much and I am sure the spouse or partner that has to sleep in it will agree☹. If you can only afford flowers that add color as an enhancement, that may be enough. The color will go through your eyes vibrating some excitement within your body and maybe healing will occur or prevent illness from even starting!

CHAPTER 27

The Magic of Prayer

*Prayer is not asking. It is a longing
of the soul. It is daily admission
of one's weakness. It is better in
prayer to have a heart without words
than words without a heart.*

MAHATMA GANDHI

W e have all questioned at one time whether God exists. I have always been a believer of God, but I have to admit that I never truly understood what believing was about completely. I knew I was protected and blessed, I knew I received answers when I needed and I knew someone had to create all that we have...the world just didn't appear without evolving no matter where and how it first started. There are so many things that made no sense to me like "ask and you shall receive" and it didn't always come. The "meek shall inherit the earth" when the bullies seemed to be holding all the cards and becoming more powerful. There just seemed to be a missing piece of information that was left out for all of it to make sense. In my heart, I knew it was true, but the dots were not connecting. So why do some prayers not get answered?

I have pondered the "what if's" until I made myself crazy: What if everyone were perfectly aligned it might be boring. What if we got everything we wanted, we might become uninterested or run out of things to want. We would have nothing to look forward to or work toward. What if God answered every prayer of ill health then no one would die until the body gives out. What would we learn, how would we experience new things and what makes it happen for some and not others? We might get stuck on a comfortable path because there is no need to shake the nest or become so complacent we take each other for granted. We may stop dreaming because we think we have all we are going to get in this lifetime.

I have always known up to this juncture of my life, that earth is a schoolroom. We actually get to choose our teachers. Of course, I am talking about life teachers. We have to take part with the "goods and the bads" of every teacher out there. We learn from both. The good nurturing advice is warming and the bad advice closes one off. Either way, we learn. I, myself, am a student of learning. I need to experience knowledge for myself. It can be the best advice in the world and I won't believe it or accept it unless I can see it work. Think of those who accept whatever they hear as truth. If the truth doesn't come from the initial source, it will never be fully the truth. It gets distorted, added to, turned around to the point that the whole story changed from the initial origin.

This leads me back to what the truth is of the "what if's"? Our original source is the unseen / Divine energy in whatever form we choose to accept it. We think of this energy as being separate from us, like a chief is to the Indian tribesman. We do not feel we can ever be at that same level and that we are not supposed to be. We believe this source is King and we are the peasants. We feel we need to hold our hand out to this energy source and ask or even beg if we really need something to happen.

We have been taught to play separate roles: Parent to child, teacher to student, boss to employee, friend to enemy, landlord to tenant. So how are we ever supposed to feel we can be closer to God, the almighty King. We were taught by prayer, but he doesn't always seem to answer. "What is wrong with me?" we say. This source must be punishing me or I am not worthy to receive. Now we are getting to the heart of why self-esteem comes into play because with higher self-esteem we are closer to the source of all. The "Me" or self-importance of needing to have all to impress others needs to be minimal to none. This is what the Divine actually wants...eliminate self-importance or take the *me, me, me* out of the question and your prayer will be answered.

So what does the Divine represent? Infinite knowledge, unlimited power, presence everywhere, perfect goodness, divine simplicity, and an immaterial existence which is selflessness and the betterment and love for all. So if you want to get closer to God you need to take the selfish ingredient out of your prayer. Easier said than done when we have been trained to just *ask and it is ours.* If you wish for this Divine energy to just give the "self" something, you are not going to get it. Even if you ask for more money for yourself to do for others, you are trying to manipulate the system and the system, *you forget,* knows all and will not be manipulated.

This Divine energy is just that. Energy. All people, animals, plants, air, other planets are connected by this energy source. One affects the other like an electrical current connecting all. It can short circuit if all is out of balance or it can run ever so smoothly when in sync. Surrender to this energy and attune to what it represents. Stop expecting this source to anoint you with all your desires when all you want is to impress and receive some kind of validation. Again, a self-esteem issue! Raise your self-esteem and you will automatically get closer to God because you will feel the energy of lightness and love that emanates those same energies back into the environment and those around you.

This Divine source does not want to be your superior. The Divine wants you to become part of this momentum, not expect "the force" to give you things like a parent gives to a child. We are used to parents running errands or come running when we are in trouble. We feel alone because we are not receiving things from God (the parent) and I think that is what we keep longing for and expect to date. It is what we have been taught. We need to just "Be" without expectation and impatience that the answer or lack of answers has disciplining values or blaming God for what you contracted for "selfishly" and did not get. This is uninformed and self-seeking. All the good and corrupt happen for a reason…period. This is why people become so tainted about belief because a prayer wasn't fulfilled. If you maintain prayer to absolve your inability to accept what is, you remain separate from this source of energy that has all to offer.

It is a choice you make, but God or Higher Source will not perpetuate your separateness from this source. In other words, the source will not shower you with your wishes if you maintain the expectation that this source will do everything for you without effort from you. Is this desire you have for your 'higher good' as we discussed in the last chapter? This is not to say you can never have material possessions because you can. To sit and expect it to materialize is not going to happen.

"All that is necessarily is to give up self-importance and allow Divine Importance to take over. You have any apprehension as to what you are surrendering to, any doubt or wonder about its sincerity, then don't surrender. It is something that comes to you when you surrender yourself to it, and it comes to you on its own volition, not by your command or demand upon it." **CA**

Reverence to this source is also needed. Ask the Divine energies: *for example* "To heal this, if it is within Thy Will, or Thy Will Be Done" in whatever the matter. Then let it go! Is it the Will of the Divine? Yes. You must accept this because a crisis may be something the Divine wishes to bring about, not as a cure, but as a destroyer. Perhaps something needs to be demolished in order that one becomes aware, recognizes a need or problem, and takes the steps necessary for modifications. If your prayer isn't appropriate to complete the universal puzzle, it may not happen the way you expected. What is the silver lining we forget to look at...Know any result is a means to re-direct you in a more appropriate way.

Letting go of self-interests, self-claims, self-pity which keep you separate from this source is not an easy task. Personal agendas do not work as I can attest to...I have not received anything I thought I wanted for myself throughout the years. It was a wall after wall after wall. I was wandering around wishing for something to happen. I had no idea what was fulfilling for me to be happy. I listened to others, majored in areas I really had no desire to do; I followed at the time because I was really separate from the source and my esteem was kept low by others who wanted control over me. I finally let go of all and just flowed!

Your plan and the Divine's plan may not jive. Knowing that the Divine is love encompassing will allow you the faith to know you will not be led astray, but toward your ultimate goal which is the best plan for your soul. If you expect to follow your plan and separate yourself from the Divine's plan, you are being selfish to the whole. It is like growing up as a child you manipulate, cry and throw tantrums to get what you want. Maybe it works if the parents fall into that trap. I have seen the end result of 'giving in' at the hospital and ultimately it isn't a pretty sight. Parents want to drop them off to be fixed because the child is out of control. "If I demand enough from them, they'll eventually give in to me and I'll get what I want!" I have seen children end their life having used this method of attaining through spite or helplessness.

There are so many little things we learn in childhood which carries over into adulthood and we try the same methods of attaining with Divine energy. You can't pull the wool over the Divine's eyes. It requires you to check yourself and dig a bit into your past to see how you have developed to attain your desires. How easily did it come and from whom? Did you walk over somebody to get it? This power seeking significance at the expense of others will meet with enough resistance over time that either life or health will fall short.

Without awareness and wisdom one's intentions and motives can get out of control. The child who needs to learn wants guidance, direction, or in some cases, discipline, in order to realign and reaffirm a new *more aware* focus. Otherwise, you just keep making the same mistakes over and over blaming others or God. You may crave power and self-significance as Hitler did. His intentions were for self in violation of God and not for the common good. He was a full on Narcissist! He grew up with an abusive father who took his problems out on the children and a mother who took no control to stop it. He never had appropriate guidance. In the end, his efforts were blocked through a series of "shocks" from other countries who desired to maintain universal harmony. *The power of the masses won.* Their combined efforts changed the course of his movement, but not without loss.

Again, loss was necessary to allow for positive future world changes. Loss in our personal lives allows for change as well. It is your choice, not God's, how you direct your choices and perceive the end results.

"The law of Co-creation states that two working in Co-creative action have the power of four working individually; and three working in Co-creative activity have the power of nine; and four working in co-creative activity have the power of sixteen; and one hundred and forty four working in harmony can change the world" CA

"So Be it. Thy Will Be Done!"
....as you see, perceive, specifically ask
and Believe.

CHAPTER 28

The Secrets of Making a Wish

Desire is the starting point of all
achievement, not a hope, not a wish,
but a keen pulsating desire which
transcends everything
NAPOLEON HILL

I cannot remember where I found this, but I believe it encompasses everything I have been talking about quite succinctly. Absorb it and Believe again! The Magic still exists!

I dwell in Deep Silence, deep within the heart of the Universe.

When making a wish, I mirror back to you whatever you wish for
with the same intensity as when you sent it forth.

So wishes are always granted.

Some wishes more powerfully than others...
and possibly not in the way you may think.

It is not a matter of whether a Real Wish will be
granted,
but a matter of you being able to receive it.

Your wish is already granted the moment you send
it to me.
You, however, must have the Power to pull it back
to you

The Power is within you, and you can use it.
There are secrets to making a wish.

There are wishes, and then there are Wishes.
(And I must be very clear – we are referring to
wishes).

A Real Wish is definitely a mighty force to be dealt
with.
A Real Wish begins deep within your heart.

Many mortals believe it won't come true, or that
they don't deserve it,

But a Real Wish is a message from your soul put there because it is supposed to happen.

Perhaps you think you just don't know How it can ever happen.
How making a wish could ever come true.

You do not need to know the How.
You only need to know the What...What you want.
The How is left to the powers of the Universe. And Me.
The How will be made known to you, if you are open.

The Wishing Star is not like a big vending machine in the sky
Where you put in a Want and it shoots out your Answer.

A granted wish does not just fall into your lap.
There will be steps you must take.

Be ready and on the alert, so they can be made known to you.
When you know what your Real Wish is it bursts forth from you like a shooting star on a beam of light straight to Me.

A Real Wish is so strong you can hardly hold it back.
You must give it the Power – from the strength of
your feelings and belief.

Your granted wish will return back to you on your
beam of light,
But beyond that, you must Expect.
Why bother making a wish if you don't Expect it to
come true?

And yet, that is the way many mortal minds work...
but not believing breaks the tie to your wish before
it even has a chance to come back to you.

Doubt, blame, impatience, all dangerously weaken
the tie to your wish
and may break it entirely.

Your wish may have even been on its way, but now
falls or fizzles out.
Then you must begin making a wish over again.

Keeping your Belief and Attention on your wish,
no matter what,
may be one of the hardest things you will ever do.

It takes tremendous will power.

That is what a Real Wish is all about.

When, you may ask, will my wish come true?
No one can say until it happens.

But remember, all things must have time to grow,
must have gestation time.

You live in the dimension of Time. I do not.

God: from Unknown Author

CHAPTER 29
Beyond Self Esteem?

We are all visitors to this time, this place. We are here just passing through. Our purpose here is to observe, to learn, to grow, to love...
....and then we return home.
AUSTRALIAN ABORIGINAL PROVERB QUOTE

I have written two other books on self-esteem hopefully for people to think and realize everyone is where they are supposed to be and everyone can take steps to begin a new path of learning. It is a choice. You can stay where you are if you are content with your results in life or you can begin to look around and see you can make changes no matter how desperate life seems to be for you. Either way, no one should be judging your choices. When you are ready to make the changes, you will make them... I repeat *when you are ready and not when others think you need to be making the changes.*

We have covered negative thoughts related to our beliefs vs. positive affirmations, health, wealth, love, and relationships with yourself and others. Self-esteem levels are based on how much you have taken time to understand your past with new focuses for your future and how it all works together to make you who you are now. My goal is to help you uncover even the simplest of slights that changed your behavior at some point and thereby affecting your decisions to date whether it worked for or against you. Some choices were made for you and some you made yourself. Each preference was made based on what you needed to learn at the time. You can always make another choice if you see it wasn't right for you. The inappropriate choices that others made for us will take a bit more digging as we assume we are either being punished for something or simply... it is what it is and we can't change... Not so.

The new age of ascending requires us to start taking responsibility for our own actions. Clearly again, there is no blame to spread to others as they were/are only doing what they knew/ know to do at the time they are doing it. We can forgive them for not knowing, but we do not have to accept the abuse or feel put upon if we allow it to continue.

There are other layers of information that you possibly will not ferret out yourselves. I, who am a forger of breaking into other realms of intelligence, will be including some data for you that you may or may not be ready to swallow. Getting yourself to a higher level of self-esteem will make me feel fulfilled, but those that ponder the following pages of data, *which can be believed or not believed,* could assist in a new reality investigation that is beyond self-esteem. It makes no difference to me if you believe as we all have choice. I personally believe all of the following as I can answer 100% "Yes" to all lists. I did not make these lists and I will try to make sure I reference where I got the information. I may not be sure who originated these lists first, but there must be at least one other person who believes as me because the lists exist.☺

This information dates back to the city of Atlantis and beyond that time. They say many of the producers/writers of sci/fy movies actually have an instinctive insight on what was and will be in order to create some of the movies we see today. Fantasy or real life? Crop circles and some of the ancient ruins have a mythical history of sorts and it is now coming to light that maybe these stories are not so mythical. We are going through a separation of worlds and eventually evil will lose the battle in the new world and remain separate from those who take the time to re-create themselves in the likeness of what our original essence truly was and will be again. This essence is peace and love for all and the manifestations of what we desire at out fingertips with just a thought. It is said we will become more telepathic. The veil between the worlds will lift and is already lifting. My path is to help assist you in taking the steps to this magical place our souls already know exist. The first step is to get your self-esteem in a good place so your thoughts can begin to manifest this place of peace inside you. This is the reason for writing my initial books. We **cannot** jump steps and self-esteem is primary.

We have to be more careful what we visualize and think because we will be manifesting much faster. This could be as simple as to wish harm on someone because they have been "in your way". You really need to take responsibility for a thought like this as it may come true even though you did not personally harm the person. Your thoughts will become reality faster. What of the person who says they really need time off from work so they can just get some sleep?

This is a true story: a man wished that very thing and ended up in a horrible motorcycle accident thereby laid up for 6 months in hospital. He got what he asked for...time off and ability to sleep. Maybe he needed to be more specific. How about a wife that wishes the spouse to learn a huge lesson for his excessive drinking and driving. Well the spouse gets a DUI and now cannot make the mortgage because he lost his job and they may now lose their home. It is all manifesting as we think it and if we are not specific on what our thoughts are, we may get something we didn't plan to get. So you see, taking responsibility for our thoughts is becoming even more necessary as this veil of the new world lifts.

The following excerpts I am including to add depth to your higher self to realize there may be more to us than the humanoid person who is floundering around down here thinking there is no purpose. The purpose is finding our way back to who we are and where we came from. I am not talking about Kansas.

THE LISTS FROM BEYOND

*Knowledge is power. Information is
liberating. Education is the premise of
progress, in every society, in every family.*
KOFI ANNAN

The forerunners for this transition, as I am one,
are here to assist you, but you have to make the effort on your own and make your own choices. We
provide the information for you and stretch your
mind to think out of the square depthless box we
have been in for so many thousands of years. I will
post the websites where I found information, but
this is by no means the only lists available. I cannot
tell you where the original lists came from or are
and maybe it is for you to research the rest on your
own. I am only compiling information for you to
start. You will know if it rings true for you and you
only. Maybe it will renew your purpose.

http://www.starchildren.info/rainbow.html

There are people who are called Indigos: I am one. I am one of the 30% here early in 50's. Please read through the list and see if anything matches you. These would be people born in 40s, 50s, and 60s.

Indigos born in the 40's, 50's and 60's are called Scouts. Here are some characteristics which I found very interesting…

"Indigo Adult Characteristics {Scouts}

Please note, anyone could have a few of these traits, but Indigo Adults have most or all of these 25 characteristics:

- Are intelligent, though may not have had top grades.
- Are very creative and enjoy making things.
- Always need to know WHY, especially why they are being asked to do something.
- Had disgust and perhaps loathing for much of the required and repetitious work in school.
- Were rebellious in school in that they refused to do homework and rejected authority of teachers, OR seriously wanted to rebel, but didn't DARE, usually due to parental pressure.

- May have experienced early existential depression and feelings of helplessness. These may have ranged from sadness to utter despair. Suicidal feelings while still in high school or younger are not uncommon in the Indigo Adult.
- Have difficulty in service-oriented jobs. Indigos resist authority and caste system of employment.
- Prefer leadership positions or working alone to team positions.
- Have deep empathy for others, yet an intolerance of stupidity.
- May be extremely emotionally sensitive including crying at the drop of a hat (no shielding) Or may be the opposite and show no expression of emotion (full shielding).
- May have trouble with RAGE.
- Have trouble with systems they consider broken or ineffective, i.e. Political, educational, medical, and legal.
- Alienation from or anger with politics – feeling your voice won't count and/or that the outcome really doesn't matter.
- Frustration with or rejection of the traditional American dream – 9-5 career, marriage, 2.5 children, house with white picket fence, etc.

- Anger at rights being taken away, fear and/ or fury at "Big Brother watching you."
- Have a burning desire to do something to change and improve the world. May be stymied what to do. May have trouble identifying their path.
- Have psychic or spiritual interest appear fairly young – in or before teen years.
- Had few if any Indigo role models. Having had some doesn't mean you're not an indigo, though.
- Have strong intuition.
- Random behavior pattern or mind style – (symptoms of Attention Deficit Disorder). May have trouble focusing on assigned tasks, may jump around in conversations.
- Have had psychic experiences, such as premonitions, seeing angels or ghosts, out of body experiences, hearing voices.
- May be electrically sensitive such as watches not working and street lights going out as you move under them, electrical equipment malfunctioning and lights blowing out.
- May have awareness of other dimensions and parallel realities.
- Sexually are very expressive and inventive OR may reject sexuality in boredom or with

intention of achieving higher spiritual connection. May explore alternative types of sexuality.

- Seek meaning to their life and understanding about the world May seek this through religion or spirituality, spiritual groups and books, self-help groups and books.
- When they find balance they may become very strong, healthy, happy individuals."

First Wave Indigo
"Knights" Profiles

These are some of the qualities and challenges that First Wave Indigos experience. Most Indigos can relate to at least 90% of this list.

- Were born en masse (about 62%) between 1969 and 1987 (With stragglers before and after - 30% were born in the 50's).
- Highly intelligent in their "Own Way."
- Are literally "wired differently" than other people.
- Know in their heart and core that they are here "on a mission" but many don't remember what that is or how to go about it.
- Have an inner awareness that what is being taught in churches and schools is NOT

accurate and know there are hidden agendas around the lies that are being accepted by the masses as "Truth." This is extremely frustrating but inspires them to uncover the cover-ups and exposed The Real Truth!

- Have a strong sense of truth, ethics, justice and freedom. (That is why "authority figures" many times irritate and frustrate them). When these are in jeopardy, will give their "all" for their cause, and many times feel they would rather die than give-in to tyranny and deception.
- Many have strong or unusual Psychic and Telekinetic abilities.
- Have extraordinary levels of compassion.
- Have purple/UV as their favorite color or see it in their dreams.
- Have an affinity to Knights, Castles, and Dragons.
- Shut down psychic abilities because it scares people.
- Feel like they could be one of the characters on the 1980's television series "The Misfits of
- Science" or one of the young people in Xavier's school for the gifted in the recent movies from the comic books "The X-Men."
- Many times get along better with animals and nature than people.

- Have a bond/connection to the trees, and nature in general.
- Can relate well to children and or the elderly.
- Feel very comfortable lounging, and would rather sit on the floor on a pillow than in a hard, uncomfortable chair. (Would prefer sitting on the floor in school, and even business meetings if they could get away with it!)
- Are very attracted to soft natural fabrics in their cloths and fuzzy blankets are the ultimate!
- Many times get very impatient when someone doesn't "get to the point."
- Creative, inventive, and very intuitive.
- Involve themselves in human/animal rights efforts.
- Have an innate sense of connectedness to all of creation - "The Web of Life." Get confused and disturbed when others don't share their reality.
- High capacity for love, and therefore others may feel uncomfortable by their intensity.
- Very sensitive, sometimes "Hyper Sensitive" and may not be able to distinguish between the emotional fields of those around them and their own personal emotions.

- May go through periods of apathy and cynicism as coping mechanisms.
- Intense longing for "their own kind" or Soul Mates, but don't know where to look.
- Have what I endearingly term H.D.D. or "Hug Deficit Disorder" and need immense amounts of physical touching, hugs, and love to "cuddle."
- Because of being misunderstood and then betrayed, may develop strong trust issues, and therefore keep many of their thoughts, feelings and opinions to themselves.
- About 30% have difficulties expressing themselves, especially in writing. NOTE: If you read some of the poorly written correspondence from some of these First Wave Indigos, you would assume they were uneducated and nearly illiterate, but the truth is, that these same people can also be speed readers and can absorb information in seconds that would take others minutes to understand and retain.
- Very disciplined when properly motivated.
- Get bored and or frustrated in school.
- Male Indigos (and many Females) for the most part don't "do authority" very well

because most of the time they are smarter than those in authority.

- Many find themselves in "Alternative Schools."
- Female Indigos seem to be able to cope better with the school systems than their male counterparts.
- Many are labeled "Dyslexic" and find themselves in "Special Classes" at school that usually never work for them.
- Indigos have a strong desire to know "why" and if they don't see "the point" in something, (or if is it isn't explained properly), will feel it is simply not worth their time/energy and will either react with resistance or just simply "blow off" the people/things that seem not worth their time and energy.
- Innately have their own ways of calculation and many have been accused of cheating in school because they do the answers in their head and cannot show their work.
- Indigos have an evolved awareness of how things work, therefore, many of the rigid rules and methods of learning Math, English, and Physics (NOT metaphysics or quantum physics) make no sense to them.

- All First wave Indigos have what might be termed as "A Gift of Healing" ....whether it is making people feel better with their humor and wit, hands on healing, animal and plant healing, healing with music and tone, or healing with new "unproven" methods.. ·some of which are natural and need no external training for.
- Many Indigos have "Telepathic Healing" abilities and long distances make no difference to the efficiency of their work.
- Because of their expanded perception, unusual creativity, wanting to try new things, and running way ahead of what is being taught in class, many were diagnosed as having Attention Deficit Disorder, and put on Ritalin as children.
- Most Indigo's (especially males) have a high innate aptitude for computers/electronics and or auto mechanics. It is common for them to "Just Know" how to operate and trouble shoot with very little help from a book or an instructor.
- First Wave Indigo's are extremely creative, and express this innate skill in many (and often times OUTRAGEOUS forms.)

These skills manifest in: Drawing, Painting, Sculpting, Decorating,

- Photography, Writing (in sometimes very extreme and unique ways), Making Blueprints and
- Prototypes, Composing and Playing Music (even if they have never had lessons), inventing games, and creating new & more efficient ways of doing things.
- Very few Indigos are interested in aggressive sports such as Football and Hockey. They would rather spend their physical exercise time and energy in personal achievement and outdoor sports such as track & field, skateboarding, mountain climbing, cycling, kayaking, etc. They are also attracted to discipline and self-defense sports such as Fencing and Martial Arts
- Because of their feeling so foreign to this planet, a very high percentage of Indigos have been put on "Antidepressants" to make them appear "Normal" and fit in our controlled society. This is just a temporary fix though, and only adds to their challenges.
- Many Indigos are drawn to Theatrics, Drama, and Stand-up Comedy. In these

WHERE IS MY MAGIC?

venues they can "pretend to be someone
else" when actually they are using this as an
outlet to vent and express their own views
and pent up emotions. It is also a place for
"misfits" to find a place of refuge and "fit
in."

- Because of their feeling so "alien" here, many
go through periods of severe grief, loneliness, and displacement ...and may turn to
drugs, alcohol, or attempt suicide for a way
out.

- One trademark that a high % of First Wave
Indigos have, is living through extreme
hardships as children, teenagers, and young
adults. Many were born into family situations that were physically, emotionally, spiritually and psychically abusive. These Indigos
had to figure out how to balance and keep
their inherent integrity levels, while being subjected to painful and life shattering
experiences.

- A large % were in planted in such horren-
dous situations as: organized crime, physical abuse, sexual abuse, and even ritual/cult
abuse & mind control. It is also common
for First Wave Indigos to have some kind of
Alien encounters.

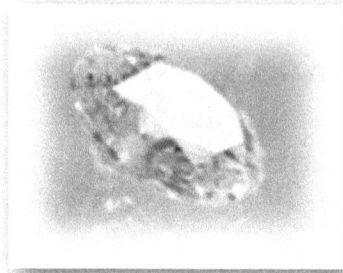

Crystals started appearing in the mid-80s.

Here are some common Crystal children characteristics and traits:

- They have big eyes.
- They have a high IQ. Many have an IQ of 160 while the average is around 130.
- They often start talking in late childhood. Usually around the age of 3. It's speculated that the reason for this is because of their telepathic abilities.
- They are very empathetic and sensitive.
- They are often (wrongly) diagnosed with ADHD.
- They are often telepathic. There have been many cases where this has been reported.
- They are careful about what they eat. They often prefer healthy meals and many are vegetarians.

- They are forgiving and often quite naive.
- They tend to have an interest in spirits, religion and the supernatural. Some say they can also see ghosts.
- Their aura has a Crystal color. This is the reason for their name.

Also:

- We are highly psychic and possess a natural lie detector.
- You can spot us by our eyes. We have large eyes that look wise beyond our years. We are old souls and even as children, we look like an old spirit in a young body. When we look at you, it feels as if we are looking into you rather that at you. This is because we are looking into you. We are reading you.
- We are often called 'serious' children. We are not. We are very playful. Our old soul shines through making people think we are serious.
- We will tolerate authority as it is the Indigo job to buck the leaders. We know that any authority we must endure is only temporary.
- We are Universal Love.
- We are gentle.

- We love to give spontaneous shows of affection.
- We are forgiveness and Oneness.
- We are Christ Consciousness.
- We are here to share the same message as Christ: Peace, Love, Forgiveness and Oneness.
- We are Empaths.
- We are highly telepathic.
- We are often misdiagnosed as having Autism or Asperger's Disorder.
- We do not begin to speak until 3 or 4 years of age. We do not need to. We only speak because YOU need us to speak. When we do decide to talk, we will usually need speech therapy as physical words are foreign to us.
- We can read your thoughts. We cannot determine between general thoughts and private thoughts. To us, there are no private thoughts. Because we cannot comprehend private thoughts, we have no understanding for personal space.
- Since we are all One, there is no such thing as personal space to us.
- Our aura is crystalline. It has soft pastel colors.

- We are natural caretaker and have natural healing abilities. We love to play and work with crystals.
- We are natural vegetarians. If we eat any meat at all, it will not be red meat.
- We often prefer the company of animals to people. As children, we prefer adults to other children.
- We will interact with other kids if they have a matching vibration. If other children do not match our vibration, we can only play for a limited time. Then, we must go back to our parents or animals to recharge.
- We observe strangers. Once we determine a person trustworthy, we show them love through hugs, kisses and words.
- We bring Crown chakra energy to the world. We are here to teach the world how to reconnect to their Divine Sacred Source. We will show you Inner Divinity.
- We open the door to telepathy which will one day be the sole source of communication to the world.
- We will incarnate into dysfunctional homes; however, we overcome karma quicker than most.

Born 2000 and above...
The Rainbow Children

- As many people might have experienced, the Rainbow children bring joy and harmony to their families. Unlike the Indigo and Crystal children, the Rainbow child is born to smile, which is accompanied by their huge hearts that are full of forgiveness.
- The Rainbow child generally recovers from the state of negative emotion quickly. This is also an important key that they hold, emotional mastery. Rainbow children are psychic and have the ability to read people's feelings. This gift is usually revealed, as they grow older.
- Rainbow Children are psychic. Beyond this and perhaps more so, they have strong wills and strong personalities. Their gifts do not stop there. They are known to be natural healers and instant manifesting ability. It is said that whatever they need or desire they can instantly manifest.
- As would be expected, they have a connection to color. In fact they resonate with the colors around them. They are drawn to color,

colorful surroundings and brightly colored clothes. Their energy is expressed in other ways too, as they are high-energy children. Their enthusiasm is demonstrated in their creativity. The Rainbow children are thought to be the builders of the New World, using Divine will.

Doreen Virtue describes characteristics of Rainbow children:

- Very few currently incarnated.
- Parents are crystal adults.
- Never incarnated before.
- No karma.
- Do not choose dysfunctional families.
- They are all about service.
- May have big eyes like the crystal children, but they are totally trusting.
- Entirely fearless of everybody.
- At a young age, the Rainbow children are able to express their needs and wants. These children actually own a great deal of personal power. Rainbow children may be misinterpreted as stubborn. However, that is our misconception.

- Rainbow children are born with knowledge on proper character integration. This will develop depending on their parents because the character integration will change if there is negative programming given to the child. As a Rainbow parent, the idea is to recognize what positive traits your Rainbow child holds.
- Rainbow children will also have immunity against junk food. Most Rainbow children are able to handle mutated cells and food products, which may result in poisoning. This is considered a very important ability, as most people may not recognize the toxins contained in junk food and the Rainbow child can take and process these types of foods with no problem. This is because of the blood that the Rainbow child carries, which has the ability to cleanse the toxins and unwanted bacteria in the food and air. So a Rainbow child may have a lot of physical clearing in the beginning stages of life. This will change once they grow older and learn how to clear ethereally or spiritually.
- Astonishingly, the Rainbow children come with no karma. Rainbow children will enjoy the life on earth learning with absolutely no strings attached to their past. This is because

they do not really continue from any previous cycle of reincarnation. This is also why they have a very high-energy frequency and physical energy.

- The rainbow child is very hyperactive. They can run the whole night and really tire you out. This is a problem that parents of Rainbow children might face.

- The purpose of the Rainbow children is to complete the final stages of the foundation that the Indigo and Crystal children have made. The three children, Indigo, Crystal, and Rainbow each have a specific task. The Indigo children are to break down the paradigm of the traditional thinking. Then the Crystal children will build their foundation on the broken paradigm. Finally, the Rainbow children are here to build on to what the Indigo and Crystal children began.

- Few writers have written on the Rainbow children because of their current status as toddlers. However, it is important to know that these children will play an important role in the earth's evolution.

- Parents of Rainbow children should understand that their children are special and parents should appreciate the gifts they have.

These gifts will help you evolve as they evolve with you.

- The rainbow children are just starting to show up on this planet, although there are already some scouts around. More Rainbow children will arrive as children of the Crystal children and also when humanity raises their vibrational frequencies and universal consciousness of the concept of oneness.

- The Rainbow children are perfectly balanced in their male and female energies. They are confident without aggressiveness; they are intuitive and psychic without effort; they are magical and can bend time, become invisible, and go without sleep and food. The Crystal children's sensitivities make them vulnerable to allergies and rashes. The angels say that the Rainbow children will have overcome this aspect...

- Rainbow children have no karma, so they have no need to choose chaotic childhoods for spiritual growth...The Rainbow children operate purely out of joy, and not out of need or Impulse. The babies will be recognized, because their energy is one of giving to parents, and not of neediness.

- Parents will realize that they cannot out-give their Rainbow children, for these children are a mirror of all actions and energy of love. Whatever loving thoughts, feelings, and actions that you send to them are magnified and returned a hundred-fold."

http://goldenageofgaia.com/2011/01/01/denise-lefay-ascension-symptoms/

ASCENSION: During the ascension process changes are occurring on all levels of your being. Ascension is a completely natural universal evolutionary process. As one shifts in vibration frequency and as our awareness expands, symptoms are experienced on the physical, mental, emotional and spiritual level. Your system is rebooting, being 'tuned up' or upgraded. Old patterns begin to fall away as one starts to embody much more light.

PHYSICAL SYMPTOMS you may notice

Ascension flu— flu-like body aches and pains but you don't get "sick" like with typical flu

Abnormal heat and/or cold in certain body parts, severe heat in bottoms of feet, cold Solar plexus etc

Hot flashes/ Kundalini risings repeatedly for both sexes

Unusual headaches that just don't go away until they are done doing what they're doing

Physical vision changes – blurring, seeing non-physical mist or fog , seeing new colors ,lights, heat mirages, warps, vortex swirls

Physical hearing changes – inner ear clicking, pressure like when you change altitude,

Hearing non-physical voices and strange sounds

Low-grade fever, chills, body and bone pains, aches and exhaustion when there's heavy
Solar and/or cosmic energies

Sudden food and chemical sensitivities that make it nearly impossible to eat a lot of foods or go much of anywhere

Insomnia and/or only being able to sleep for an hour or two and then waking up repeatedly throughout the night

Drastically less dreaming (because you're dealing with issues/energies 24/7/365 we're transmuting while awake too)

Sudden diarrhea (usually after you've been through a hard phase of transmuting lower Energies and then shifting into a higher state)

Sudden nausea or "morning sickness" for both sexes

Weird food cravings, repeated high protein cravings (due to increased transmuting of energies), need for a lot of food fuel

Severely increased sense of smell, smelling strange smells for days, weeks or months even (like burning incense or smoke)

Sense that your bones are not as dense and solid as they were in lower 3D, they now feel more like cartilage that can bend etc.

Profound exhaustion, feeling profound exhaustion and physical pains and aches after having been out in the lower world for a couple of hours,

feel better once you return to your higher vibrating home/land/space etc.
Internal electrical-like vibrations or buzzing of the "rewiring" process

Super sensitivity to sounds, light, sunlight, even movement, dizziness, sense of spinning or tipping over or dropping through the floor

EMOTIONAL SYMPTOMS

Crying over simple things that profoundly move you, crying over the stupidity, crying because you feel SO much (this is 5D Heart Consciousness beginning)

Rage and deep anger over the stupidity, anger/rage/frustration over everything and everyone still in a lower energy and state of awareness. They're literally too painful physically and emotionally to be around or to endure now

Sudden and total intolerance of anything, anyone, any system, religion, government, foods, belief systems etc. Intolerance of anything vibrating lower than you currently are

Sense of being very alone and on your own with no one else around you who understands what's really happening to reality and you

Needing to be alone and isolated from other people

Ultra-sensitive emotionally – like puberty/pregnancy/menopause all happening at the same time!

Emotionally knowing and feeling things in other people that you never could perceive prior

Family issues and "stuff" that must be dealt with within yourself and your bodies

Total emotional disconnect with things and people you used to love and enjoy very much
Feeling like you are changing so profoundly that you're actually dying (you are and it's part of this process)

MENTAL SYMPTOMS

Sudden loss of mental focus and ability to concentrate

Sudden inability to read books due to inability to focus, concentrate, or even comprehend what you're trying to read!

Forgetting the names of common everyday things, objects, places, people etc. – like "milk", "hammer", "orange", etc.
Forgetting your own name and/or sense of old familiar "you" or "self"

Having to triple check things because you can't remember if you actually did them or just thought about doing it

Loosing track of "time", loosing track of yourself within "time", suddenly not knowing

What time of the year it is or even what year it is!

Thinking and physically doing things becomes very blurred to your awareness, feeling disconnected from things like never before

Disconnect with the ego self that was mentally multitasking constantly, inability to focus and so you relax and un focus finally

PSYCHIC SYMPTOMS

Seeing, hearing, feeling, sensing nonphysical beings both positive and negative,

Perceiving strange unknown energies and lights

Hearing nonphysical voices call your name

Seeing different colored lights, balls, points of brilliant light, flash and roll around in your house and/or outside

Seeing solid 3D objects (like walls etc) suddenly look like a heat mirage, sparkle, shimmer with brilliant light and appear transparent

Seeing, hearing, and even telepathy with both "positive" and "negative" beings, entities

Perceiving areas of condensed negative energy

Negative psychic attacks by other lower vibrating living humans, and/or negative non-physical energies, beings etc. (deal with it and move on. It's someone's unresolved negative shit looking for a new place to live; transmute it, release it all and move on) working through polarity resolution, repeated encounters with polarized energies, polarized consciousness, etc.

Seeing, hearing, feeling, smelling, sensing higher positive non-physical Beings, Guides

ETs, Angelics, other Lightworkers, other Starseeds etc.

Increasing conscious connection and awareness with your Higher Self – spherical or "triality consciousness" instead of the old 3D polarized and linear consciousness

Increasing but HIGHER empathy, telepathy, clairvoyance, greater and greater unity within yourself and with other people that are vibrating at or near the same frequency and state of ascension that you are, 5D awareness or Heart consciousness

Coming under negative psychic attacks occasionally from both human and nonhuman

Energies, thankfully decreasing in potency over the months and years

Stages of dreamless sleeping, stages of numerous unpleasant nightmares each night for weeks at a time. This usually happens when we're making yet another shift and need to process some more stuff and energies within ourselves.

Accelerated symptoms:

http://www.sandrawalter.com/accelerated-ascension-symptoms/

- Triple digits: every time you glance at a digital clock it has double or triple digits. 1:11, 2:22, 3:33, 4:44, 8:55 (just glanced, there it is), etc. All day long. This can be fun or maddening depending on your perspective. It's just the higher levels saying *hello* or *pay attention.*
- Breaking free from restrictive jobs, life-styles, disharmonious people or situations. Sometimes it is conscious, sometimes your higher self will do it for you.
- Desire to simplify belongings, lifestyle, habits
- Heightened awareness, mystical experiences, increased synchronicity
- Breaking the false membrane between the solar plexus and heart center. You'll know when it occurs.

- Feelings of tremendous joy, love and compassion: when the lower and higher chakras begin to unite
- Full-on Kundalini risings: bliss-gasms become a regular occurrence
- Skin eruptions: occasional unusual rashes, bumps – purification of emotion, toxins, imbalances
- Beings in your peripheral vision; floating veils, shadowy figures, white objects
- Seeing particles of light all the time
- Seeing auras or vortexes of energy around plants, animals, people
- Episodes of clairvoyance, clairaudience, clairsentience, Clair cognizance
- White noise, ringing, electronic-type noise or tones in the ears becomes more intense, sensing messages within the sounds
- Creativity bursts: receiving creative inspirations at an overwhelming rate
- Impatience: You want to get on with the process faster than your body can adjust. It's just your mind, pay attention to what is holding you back form experiencing more. Sometimes the impatience itself is the block.

- Teachers start to appear to assist you on your journey: people, movies, books, events, Mother Earth, Father Sun, Star family
- Consuming interest in self-knowledge and creativity: expressing one's true nature in work and play
- Deeper understanding of spiritual truths
- Higher perspective becomes habitual: compassion for all journeys, honoring all paths
- Third eye opening, clarifying
- Akashic access: understanding your past journeys here, seeing the lessons.
- Journeys in meditation become intense and purposeful: crystalline cities, geometry, grid work, star gate travel
- Feeling the Observer or Witness consciousness, separation from 3D constructs
- Desire to serve from the heart
- Deep understanding of Mother Earth and Humanity's journey
- Desire for mastery of your consciousness

CHAPTER 30

Where Is Our Magic *In Summary*

"The whole secret of existence
is to have no fear.
Never fear what will become of
you, depend on no one.
Only the moment you reject
all help are you freed."
BUDDHA

I am always curious about the number of chapters written per each of my books as everything has meaning and magic for me! The number 30 seems to be the magic numeral this time! I have researched the number 30 to mean: 'People will do well when given the freedom to express and live with a zest for life'! The zest for life has been silenced in most people. People are tired of, people tolerate and people oblige the dysfunctions in others just because they have been in our lives for so long. We repress our true thoughts for fear of hurting others and yet we allow them to hurt us. In the end, we are only hurting ourselves and snuffing the zest out of our own lives.

Thirty is also a well liked number because it represents the creation of good times with delightful laughs. We need to review if we are really enjoying life or if we feel life has handed us a bad deck of cards. What person or situation makes us recoil every time we have to face one or the other? When is the last time you truly had a belly laugh? It is all in the attitude of our perception and choice!

Life is meant to be enjoyed! If we are not enjoying life, whether it is because of a person or situation, what would we change and why are we not making changes? Life flows by with or without us as a river flows. When the flow stops or dries up a stagnant pond remains… and does what? It becomes stinky and infested with mosquitoes. It may even become poisonous. If you feel your life is on track, but everyone around is making you miserable with malicious disrespect of your boundaries and it continues even after you ask politely; maybe it is time to shed the old skin that has been annoying, chaffing or itching you. I mean this figuratively and realistically.

Four months of the year have 30 days and it would seem each of those is a beginning cycle of a seasonal change. These months are September, April, June and November! Seasons always follow the same cycle every year. Every season closes with a transition into the next season and always with a chance at a new beginning. We can view the same colors and scents or we can transition with something new. You can look back at what has worked or not and then look forward to anticipated new possibilities. We parallel nicely with nature in so many ways. Coincidence?

In this book, I have included many diverse and unique possibilities of what exists at our fingertips which can aide us in making changes easier. It may be color enhancements, simply effort and direction, emotional adjustments, prayer or even magically making a wish and believing it will come true! I hope to have bundled together a few missing pieces that have been hidden blocks of failure for all of us and how the old and new beliefs guide us whether in alignment with our thoughts or not. Our direction is there by what we choose to see.

We spend much wasted energy trying to understand what appears beyond our reach because we keep comparing ourselves to others and allowing their expectations to affect what we think about ourselves. People will abuse these expectations as well. They will make promises and paint a great picture keeping you out of your alignment with their false aspirations. Our boundaries need to be strong and specific to keep us safe and on track. If we are out of alignment with ourselves we cannot expect the universe to help us achieve our dreams!

There really is nothing in my books that is new information. All knowledge started somewhere long before me or anyone else in my same timeline. We talk about how our past connection with Greek and Roman cultures had to be the beginning of our wisdom and learning, but we can't fill in the blank as to how they acquired their knowledge. There is a beginning and end to all, the alpha and the omega, as Jesus described of himself. Depending on your belief, and I am not asking you to label yourself with a specific icon, but realize we need to open our minds past what we have been able to touch and experience to date. Self-esteem is also something one cannot touch, but we can know and feel that it exists and in what manner it lives or not. Does I feel good or not?

Perhaps Chapter 29 is an intangible possibility for where we started (The Lists) and how we have been assisted to get where we are now. The question then arises as to where the ET's began? Is there a beginning or is it simply an infinite source that is tapped into as we grow and become ready for it. Do we even need to know the answer and what answer do we seek? Maybe it is all a journey to see what we can accomplish in a certain amount of time with as many obstacles to overcome as we can create. What would happen if we stopped creating obstacles and found out freedom and love were already present? Love should never be used as a weapon to control others and we all know this, so why do we let it continue? Seek out the love which already exists inside you which makes you feel magically at peace. When you do, the weapon becomes a wand!

We can pinpoint where this body started and one day it will end. What lies in between that time is for you to decide and make a wise choice with or without the dysfunctional aura that looms over all of us. We can continue to believe we are ruled by our past within limited possibilities or believe there may be other potential possibilities we have yet to see or experience. Everyone is where they are supposed to be...as stated earlier in my book by a Cosmic Awareness we may never meet, but we can feel exists because the words feel correct: Most definitely worth repeating a second time:

... *"Realize that each individual is at the exact place they need to be. That friends and family may not perceive as you do, may not understand as you do, that this tremendous leap forward has occurred. Do not try to convince them, do not argue with them, for it is not perhaps their journey and they may sabotage yours. Instead, live your own life ...focus on creating your inner reality and allow this process to be that which is your stance alone, your presentation to others. You do not need to debate others that you are correct, that there is something happening, for all are immersed in their own perspective reality. There is no need to teach those who are closed, those who are not teachable, but as you live your life you become the strong architect of your new reality. Those who have a capacity to learn and grow will see your truth will understand there is something different about your reality and how you manifest your reality. This is my goal to help assist you to your new reality if you are open and choose to change." Cosmic Awareness*

Everyone's magic is created by the intensity of thoughts that come from within our own heart and mind. What we give most thought to is what manifests. There are endless possibilities of what one can create through effort and belief that your dreams are already part of your reality ... minus the doubts....My goal is to expand your thinking, not change you. You can believe or not. If each person was equal and our role was chosen for us, there would be no adventure or emotion. We still have choice to follow our own path and you choose how you follow it☺. The fact we have choice is magical!

Everyone has dark moments in their life. Use your dreams during this time and hold that as your focus until you can find and secure your footing. The one thing you can do alone and quietly is read. Your imagination can still function and no one can take that away permanently. Your magic exists even though many will attempt to snuff out those embers of hope. Listen in the darkness to your own voice. Your intuitional energies will not communicate with words, but through energy which we equate to feelings. Combine this energy with follow through and the more your life will start to look like a series of amazing "coincidences." The intensity of your will to thoughts on something activates "exactly" what you think into existence...

Be good to yourself first and live with integrity!

About The Author

Joanne Salsbury was born in Portsmouth, Ohio. Portsmouth is a small southern Ohio River town nestled within a state forest of prominent Native American heritage. She grew up knowing the land and the peace it can bring as well as the education of life beyond the books. She gained education in Europe and finalized her degrees at the University of Cincinnati.

Presently, she is living in San Diego, California where she works in behavioral health administration. Joanne was self employed for twelve years as an organizational consultant... restructuring companies toward a new conclusion of a high self-esteem persona. She has done extensive public speaking and seminars for the individual as well as for companies.

Joanne is writing to all people in the world with hope that each person realizes that he/she can achieve high self-esteem no matter your education, circumstances or background. High self-esteem is a personal issue between you and your higher good. It is learned behavior that is compiled from all of your experiences and interactions and refined over time to paint that picture of yourself that you can love unconditionally.

Our natural emotions have been distorted in value over time and Joanne would like to help you remember and gain back the understanding and purpose of your own emotions, so you can have your individual self-esteem back as well. Look beyond and know what dreams you feel and envision are valid. Bring back the magic because it still exists and never really left us!

www.ingramcontent.com/pod-product-compliance
Lightning Source LLC
Chambersburg PA
CBHW031126090426

42738CB00008B/983